OECD Public Governance Reviews

Open Government in Tunisia: La Marsa, Sayada and Sfax

This work is published under the responsibility of the Secretary-General of the OECD. The opinions expressed and arguments employed herein do not necessarily reflect the official views of OECD member countries.

This document, as well as any data and any map included herein, are without prejudice to the status of or sovereignty over any territory, to the delimitation of international frontiers and boundaries and to the name of any territory, city or area.

Please cite this publication as:
OECD (2019), *Open Government in Tunisia: La Marsa, Sayada and Sfax*, OECD Public Governance Reviews, OECD Publishing, Paris, *https://doi.org/10.1787/9789264310995-en*.

ISBN 978-92-64-31098-8 (print)
ISBN 978-92-64-31099-5 (pdf)

OECD Public Governance Reviews
ISSN 2219-0406 (print)
ISSN 2219-0414 (online)

The statistical data for Israel are supplied by and under the responsibility of the relevant Israeli authorities. The use of such data by the OECD is without prejudice to the status of the Golan Heights, East Jerusalem and Israeli settlements in the West Bank under the terms of international law.

Photo credits: Cover © designed by Mohamad Sabra, based on images available on Shutterstock (© Mashhour, © Efesenko @Habub M'henni).

Corrigenda to OECD publications may be found on line at: *www.oecd.org/about/publishing/corrigenda.htm*.

Foreword

Since 2011, Tunisia has reformed its legal and policy frameworks to give greater autonomy to local government and promote open and inclusive government at both national and subnational levels. While the reforms give citizens a more active role in policy making, they also require profound changes to Tunisia's governance culture, policies and practices. In this context, some Tunisian municipalities and citizens have already introduced innovative open government initiatives and created partnerships with civil society.

Taking stock of these experiences, this report analyses the legal and institutional frameworks for open government policies and practices at the local level based on three pilot municipalities, La Marsa, Sayada and Sfax. It assesses their frameworks and practices against best practices in OECD countries and with regard to the Recommendation of the OECD Council on Open Government. The report acknowledges the efforts undertaken by these three municipalities to transform their relationship with citizens and makes recommendations for taking a more comprehensive and structured approach to open government.

In addition, in the light of Tunisia's ongoing transition and decentralisation process, it offers recommendations to the central government for creating adequate structures, resources and procedures for open government at the local level.

This report was prepared at the request of Tunisia's central and local government authorities. It seeks to assist Tunisia in implementing Article 139 of the Constitution, which provides for participatory democracy and the principles of open government for local authorities.

The OECD, under its MENA-OECD Governance Programme, has been helping Tunisia develop and implement public policies that promote transparency, stakeholder participation, integrity and accountability since 2012.

It is hoped that the results of this work will inspire not only other Tunisian municipalities, but communities around the world to implement open government initiatives.

Acknowledgements

The OECD Secretariat wishes to express its gratitude to all those who made this report possible. First and foremost, thanks are due to the Government of Tunisia, in particular to the Presidency of the Government, the Ministry of Local Affairs and Environment and the municipalities of La Marsa, Sayada and Sfax, for their constant support during the various workshops and peer review missions for this project. The OECD would also like to extend its gratitude to all the other stakeholders from civil society and the private sector – who took part in the peer review.

In addition, the OECD would like to thank the public officials who served as peer reviewers: Guy Grenier (Montreal, Canada), Fréderic Benhaim (Paris/ Ile-de-France Region, France) and Paul-Henri Philips (Brussels Region, Belgium).

This report was prepared by the Directorate for Public Governance at the OECD, headed by Marcos Bonturi, as part of the MENA-OECD Governance Programme. It falls within the framework of the "Open Government" project, managed by the Governance Reviews and Partnerships Division, under the responsibility of Martin Forst. The report was produced under the strategic direction of Alessandro Bellantoni, head of the Open Government Unit. The peer review and drafting process was led by policy analyst Katharina Zuegel. The report was written by Katharina Zuegel, with support and contributions from Paqui Santonja, project co-ordinator and policy analyst. Caroline Rolland-Diamond provided editorial support and Roxana Glavanov was responsible for layout and proofreading. Administrative support was provided by Michelle Ortiz.

The report was developed in line with the mandate to promote open government reforms in the MENA region, received by the OECD within the context of the G7 Deauville Partnership with Arab Countries in Transition. The OECD wishes to thank the Middle East Partnership Initiative (MEPI) of the United States for its financial support.

Table of contents

Tables

Figures

Boxes

Follow OECD Publications on:

 *http://twitter.com/OECD_Pubs*

 *http://www.facebook.com/OECDPublications*

 *http://www.linkedin.com/groups/OECD-Publications-4645871*

 *http://www.youtube.com/oecdilibrary*

OECD Alerts *http://www.oecd.org/oecddirect/*

Acronyms and abbreviations

ARP	Assembly of the Representatives of the People
CPSCL	Loans and Support Fund for Local Authorities
HAICA	High Independent Authority of the Audio-visual Commission
OGP	Open Government Partnership
AIP	Annual Investment Plan
PDUGL	Urban Development and Local Government Programme
MIP	Municipal Investment Plan

Executive Summary

An opportunity to implement open government practices at the local level

Tunisia has been undergoing a period of transition and evolution of its political system since 2011, leading to reforms of its legal and policy frameworks. These reforms promote open government practices through increased transparency, participation and accountability. Tunisia's membership in the Open Government Partnership is proof of this commitment. The 2014 Constitution, which enshrines the principles of a democratic, republican and participatory regime, as well as the principles of self-government (*libre administration*), participatory democracy and open governance for local authorities, offers an opportunity to implement open government practices at the local level. The ongoing decentralisation process is seen as going hand-in-hand with more open, participatory and accountable governance. Local authorities are therefore called upon to play a stronger role in local development by bringing public policies closer to citizens. This presents a challenge at a moment of transition and uncertainty in terms of legal and institutional frameworks and available resources. Yet, the role and legitimacy of local authorities have already increased since the local elections of 6 May 2018.

Local open government practices in the context of national efforts

Since 2011, the transition government has been engaged in creating the necessary conditions for a profound cultural shift in the governance system, the role of the state and citizens' rights. The objective is a system that is more transparent, more open and more participatory. These reforms at national level, such as adoption of the Constitution and of a law on access to information, membership in the Open Government Partnership (OGP) and the Urban Development and Local Government Programme (PDUGL) have a significant impact on open government reforms at local level. The second OGP action plan highlights the importance of open government at the local level, while the PDUGL calls for a participatory approach to prepare Annual Investment Plans. There is thus a need for greater co-ordination between initiatives at central and local levels in order to promote the adoption of open government practices by local authorities while providing them with the means to implement these policies and align them with their own initiatives.

Open government in the context of an on-going decentralisation process

The decentralisation provided for in Chapter 7 of the 2014 Constitution is a response to the lack of local democracy and the limited capacity of municipalities to develop their territories. It enshrines concepts such as local government, decentralisation and self-government. While the principles of decentralisation were recently defined by the adoption, on 26 April 2018, of the Code for Local Authorities, municipalities are still governed by older laws, and were managed until the recent local elections of May 2018 by appointed special delegations. Confronted with citizens' expectations, municipalities are now being called upon to introduce innovative approaches to designing public policies. In collaboration with citizens and civil society, and inspired by the practices of some Tunisian municipalities, local governments should identify open government practices to implement while preparing for the adoption of the principles outlined in the new Code for Local Authorities.

Open government in La Marsa, Sayada and Sfax

While awaiting local elections and the implementation of the decentralisation reform, several municipalities, including La Marsa, Sayada and Sfax, took the initiative to create a more open and citizen-centred local administration. La Marsa and Sfax are among the few municipalities that adopted participatory budgeting. As for Sayada, the municipality is engaged in a partnership with civil society to make the municipality more transparent. These initiatives have helped to build a climate of trust between the municipalities, their citizens and the civil society organisations involved in the process. These municipalities are therefore to be congratulated for the manner in which they have introduced open government practices.

Nevertheless, challenges remain for implementing the principles of open government at the local level. The institutional, human and financial frameworks will need long-term adjustment in order to respond to the new demands of the legal framework and of citizens for local development. Implementing the law on access to information requires a focus on training. In addition, participatory initiatives could be extended to large-scale municipal projects, such as urban development plans. The Code for Local Authorities, which sets out a great many mechanisms for transparency, participation and accountability and recognises the importance of citizens, civil society and the media to municipal affairs could serve to create an open government vision and strategy for municipalities. Harnessing this would further consolidate the efforts of municipalities, together with those of civil society, to break with the culture of a closed administration and establish new mechanisms for interaction.

Introduction

The revolution of 14 January 2011 began in Tunisia's poorest regions. It cast a spotlight on the difficulties faced by Tunisians based on their area of origin, and their frustration at the lack of opportunities and economic development in the interior regions (The European Union's Committee of the Regions 2014). Seven years later, the development of the interior regions remains at the core of popular demands, and the implementation of the decentralisation provided for in the 2014 Constitution is eagerly awaited (OECD, 2017a). Since 2011, the municipalities – administrations that are traditionally close to citizens – have been faced with growing calls and demands from the people for increased socio-economic development and the establishment of local democracy.

The 2014 Constitution enshrines the principles of a democratic, republican and participatory regime, and it confirms the strengthening of local authorities, managed according to the principle of self-government. It also stipulates that local authorities should operate according to the principle of open governance (Article 139) and must therefore systematically put in place open government policies. As a result, it offers municipalities the conditions to enable them to play a more prominent role in local development, and it also offers citizens a greater role in this same development. Since 2011, municipalities have been attempting to respond to these expectations by introducing new practices to interact with citizens. For their part, citizens and organised civil society are demanding their newly acquired civic and political freedom, calling for greater transparency and participation, while proposing open government practices to the municipalities. This engagement on the part of municipalities and their citizens has led to the emergence, albeit sporadically, of open government practices and initiatives at the local level.

Tunisia is currently undergoing a period of transition and evolution of its political system: the country is moving from a regime that was characterised by a unitary state, in which central government wielded power over the local authorities, but for which it exhibited negligible competencies, to a system in which there is greater autonomy for the municipalities, together with the promotion of local democracy and a closer relationship between citizens, the administration and its public services. This report has been prepared in the context of this development, and it presents an analysis of the current situation of open government at the local level in Tunisia. Tunisia's open government team, in collaboration with the Ministry of Local Affairs and Environment, selected the municipalities of La Marsa, Sayada and Sfax for a pilot study, since these have adopted mechanisms for transparency and citizen participation. The study aims to disseminate best practices and draw up recommendations that will enable the implementation of constitutional provisions and create the conditions for inclusive and sustainable social and economic development of municipalities. The report was written during a period of transition[1] and therefore evaluates an exceptional situation that is expected to change following adoption of the Code for Local Authorities, and in the wake of the first local elections of May 2018; however, it is ultimately based on the experiences of open government in Tunisia during these past seven years, and the lessons learned from them may reveal the path to follow in order to help municipalities become more transparent, more inclusive and more open.

An opportunity to implement open government practices at the local level

The current context offers an opportunity to foster a new culture of open governance at the local level, based on proximity and constant dialogue for better local development, designed and constructed as closely as possible with the citizens themselves (OECD, 2017a). The on-going decentralisation process is considered as going hand in hand with a more open, more participatory and more accountable governance, since it highlights the importance of local democracy and the development of public policies that are better aligned with citizens' needs.

A number of legal texts containing provisions conducive to open government have been adopted. Indeed, the legal framework leaves municipalities with no choice but to adopt principles and mechanisms for open government. Article 139 of the Constitution stipulates that "local authorities shall adopt the mechanisms of participatory democracy and the principles of open governance to ensure broader participation by citizens and civil society in the preparation of development programmes and land management and monitoring of their implementation, in accordance with the law." The Code for Local Authorities highlights this choice, dedicating an entire chapter (Chapter 5) to participatory democracy and open governance, and creating new committees within municipal councils for participatory democracy and open governance on the one hand, and for media, communication and evaluation on the other (Article 210). In addition, a number of reforms to the national legal and policy framework introduce obligations and mechanisms for open government. Significant reforms in this regard include organic law no. 2016-22 of 24 March 2016 on the right to access to information, which also applies to local authorities (Art. 2), the Urban Development and Local Government Programme (PDUGL), which seeks to implement constitutional provisions linked to decentralisation, the adoption of mechanisms for participatory democracy and the principle of self-government of municipalities (discussed in detail below), and commitment number 4 on transparency and open government at the local level in Tunisia's second national action plan for open government.

The municipalities, whose competencies will be reinforced by the on-going reform, and whose legitimacy has increased since the elections of May 2018, should serve as a driver for local development. They are called upon to develop and implement mechanisms for participatory democracy and open governance, which enable them to better respond to demands for local development.

References

OECD (2017a), Un meilleur contrôle pour une meilleure gouvernance locale en Tunisie : Le contrôle des finances publiques au niveau local, Examens de l'OCDE sur la gouvernance publique, OECD Publishing, Paris, http://dx.doi.org/10.1787/9789264265967-fr.

Notes

[1] Note: The interviews with the three municipalities were held in February and March 2017, and preparation of the report was based on data collected until May 2018.

Chapter 1. National initiatives for open government at the local level

This chapter situates open government at the local level in Tunisia in the context of the reforms undertaken by the central government. It analyses open government reforms at the central level and their impact on local authorities, while evaluating the involvement of local authorities in these reforms, and in the structures that manage them.

The OECD's concept of open government at the local level

Local administrations are the foundations of the State, the interface through which citizens enter into contact with public policy. "The proximity of citizens and the state spurs engagement, but also shapes citizens' perception about the government. Thus, it is not surprising that cities, regions or provinces have, in the last decades, been places for citizen engagement. The demands for greater engagement of citizens in urban planning date back to the 60/70s. Innovative and interactive approaches to involve citizens in policy making arose in parallel with the decentralisation efforts initiated by many countries from the 1970s and consisted of transferring authority, responsibility and resources from the national government to lower governmental levels, to better respond to citizens' needs and demands" (OECD, 2016a).

Local administrations have remained central to initiatives for more transparent, more open, more participatory and more accountable governance. Indeed, a wave of new municipal initiatives for citizen engagement and transparency has emerged, largely as a result of the opportunities offered by information and communication technologies. Direct contact between the municipality and its citizens remains an important channel for inclusion and dialogue, and a key factor that distinguishes open government initiatives at the local level from those at the national level. In addition, the relevance and proximity of municipal affairs to citizens' daily lives, and the impact that they have on these – for example, in the areas of urban transport and land-use planning – change the ways in which people participate, and they can in general make public participation easier.

According to the OECD, "open government is a culture of governance that promotes the principles of transparency, integrity, accountability and stakeholder participation in support of democracy and inclusive growth" (OECD, 2017a). To achieve open government, national and local administrations must adopt a new culture of governance, which simultaneously requires a strong political will, a consistent whole-of-government approach, human and financial resources, and appropriate institutions and practices. There are a number of objectives that drive countries to adopt open government initiatives (see Figure 1.1) (OECD, 2016a).

Figure 1.1. Objectives of national open government strategies

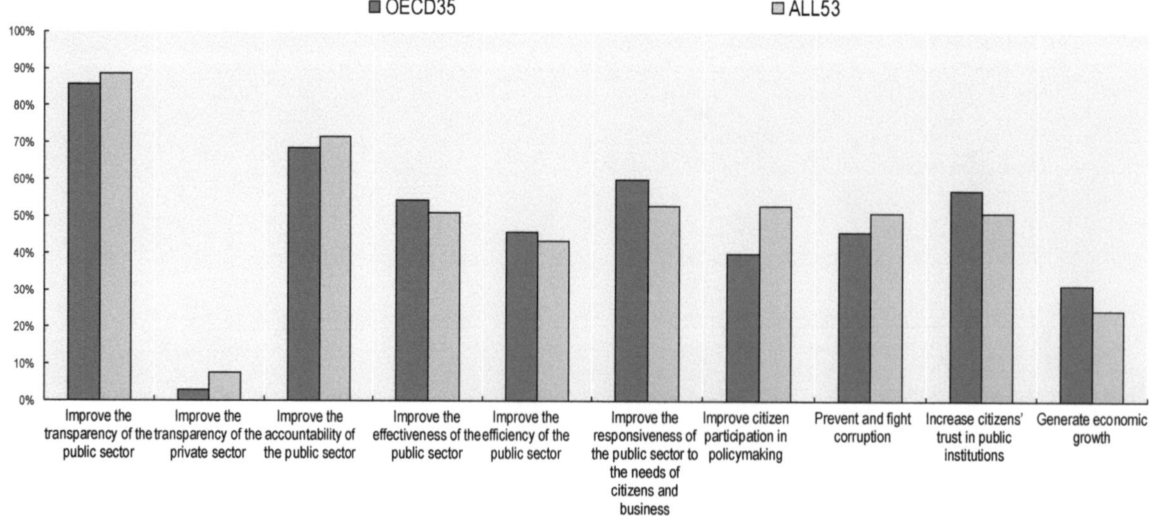

Source: OECD, 2016a.

Thanks to the Open Government Partnership (OGP), a movement has developed worldwide to promote open government by targeting national administrations. Today, more than 70 countries, including Tunisia, are already engaged in implementing open government practices. However, the participation of local administrations in this dynamic remains weak. Only about 40% of the 12 OECD countries that have implemented a coordinating mechanism to promote open government have included local government representatives in the mechanism (OECD, 2016a). In Tunisia, local government is not included in the national steering committee that has been set up to elaborate the country's open government policy. Local administrations are, however, well positioned to interact with citizens and understand their needs. Open government at the local level will help to bring the public authorities closer to the citizens, design policies that are better suited to the needs of local communities, and, as a result, promote a more effective achievement of policy objectives throughout the country. In this regard, it is essential that local administrations remain at the heart of open government initiatives, a principle that the Tunisian Constitution recognises under Article 139. Furthermore, including local administrations in the open government programme will enable the country to come closer to what the OECD defines as an Open State. According to the OECD Recommendation, an Open State is a situation "when the executive, legislature, judiciary, independent public institutions, and all levels of government - recognising their respective roles, prerogatives, and overall independence according to their existing legal and institutional frameworks - collaborate, exploit synergies, and share good practices and lessons learned among themselves and with other stakeholders to promote transparency, integrity, accountability, and stakeholder participation, in support of democracy and inclusive growth".

The open government movement in Tunisia

Transparency, participation, accountability and an end to corruption were at the heart of the demands that citizens made in 2011. From the beginning of its mandate, the transition government pledged to create conditions for a profound cultural shift in governance, the role of the state, and the rights of citizens to establish a more transparent, more open and more participatory system of governance (OECD, 2016b). Examples include the adoption of a decree-law on access to administrative documents and a decree-law on associations in 2011, the liberalisation of the media, and the introduction of the new press code. At the same time, civil society has relentlessly demanded and fought for its rights and civil liberties, particularly when security considerations and challenges have prevailed[1].

Open government has appeared to be a promising pathway to meet the challenge of regaining citizens' confidence, with the aim of ensuring their contribution to and participation in the decision-making process. Indeed, the concept of open government is based on a culture of governance rooted in transparency, integrity, accountability and stakeholder participation (OECD, 2017a), a culture that is aligned with the principles of the 2014 Constitution and which breaks with that of the former regime. As a result, the government, working together with civil society, the private sector and the legislature, has undertaken substantial reforms that have brought about remarkable transformations, such as improvements in budgetary transparency. These reforms have received international recognition, since Tunisia's membership in the Open Government Partnership (OGP) in 2014.

Supported by the OECD, Tunisia launched a process of dialogue within the public administration, as well as with civil society, to promote the principles of open government and to participate in the OGP in 2012[2]. Currently, a Joint Consultative Committee, made up of representatives of the different ministries and civil society, is responsible for developing, implementing and monitoring national biennial action plans that include Tunisia's priority initiatives for open government. These plans are among the requirements for participating in the OGP, which also requires an independent evaluation of the action plans, as well as a participatory approach to their development (OECD, 2016b). At the time of writing this report, Tunisia is implementing its second action plan for 2016-2018. This procedure has promoted the adoption of a culture of open dialogue, based on trust between government and civil society involved in the OGP process; this already represents a good practice and may inspire other open government initiatives. In addition, participation in the OGP has helped to spread the culture and principles of open government within part of the public administration, which is the engine for reforms[3].

The open government movement goes beyond the OGP process. According to information received from civil society, discussions are under way in Parliament, in consultation with civil society, to introduce the principles of open government into parliamentary methods and operations. Aside from La Marsa, Sayada and Sfax, a number of municipalities have also developed open government initiatives. These include activities aimed at encouraging dialogue between society and government. Roundtables have been organised in Kasserine and Sidi Bouzid to enable a tripartite discussion to take place between local authorities, representatives of the private sector and representatives of civil society, as well as initiatives seeking to ensure that citizens' priorities are taken into greater account through participatory budgeting in Gabès (GIZ, 2014).

Open government practices in Tunisia are also emerging as the result of a civil society that is both active and expert on issues of transparency, citizen participation and accountability. Initiatives include the parliamentary observatory project 'Marsad', launched by the association *Al Bawsala*, which has succeeded in bringing transparency to the activities of Parliament and its members; the activities of the association *IWatch* that is encouraging a culture of integrity, mainly among youth, and supporting whistle-blowers; and *YouthDecides*, which fosters the participation of young people in public debate. However, most of the organisations working in this area are based in Tunis, and they only represent a small part of the civil society. Nevertheless, these associations have and continue to play a decisive role in consolidating and implementing a system of governance based on transparency, integrity, accountability, and stakeholder participation. (For a full discussion of open government initiatives at the national level and recommendations, see Box 1.1 and OECD, 2016b, Open Government in Tunisia).

Box 1.1. Excerpt: Recommendation of the Open government Review of Tunisia

Organising for Open Government reform at the centre of government

- Provide high-level leadership and co-ordination.

- Establish on-going working-level structures for implementation.

- Develop a strategy for each area, including resources required for implementation and performance measures to assess progress.

- Extend Open Government to the local level.

- Assess progress on Open Government regularly, with stakeholder participation.

Citizen engagement

- Establish a formal steering group to implement access to information and an institution to ensure the application of the norms.

- Fully implement press and media freedoms.

- Develop and institutionalise a Tunisian approach to citizens' engagement.

- Promote the formation of civil society networks to organise and broaden engagement.

- Expand the capacity of the government to follow up on citizens' engagement initiatives.

Budget transparency

- Improve availability of budget information by publishing all of the reports named by the OECD guidelines on this issue in a timely manner.

- Prepare and provide a broader set of background and analytic materials to accompany the budget and guide the budget debate.

- Strengthen the capacity of the Assembly to examine the budget, fully participate in budgetary discussions and analyse budget performance.

- Reinforce the government's audit capacity.

- Establish a detailed fiscal transparency action plan incorporating these measures.

Integrity and the fight against corruption

- Fully implement the code of ethical conduct for government employees.

- Reform the asset declaration system to reinforce its efficiency.

- Fully implement the TUNEPS e-procurement system.

- Fully implement a whistle-blowers protection system.

- Provide adequate resources for the audit and performance evaluation functions.

Information and communication technologies (ICT)

- Strengthen human and financial resources available to the government in ICTs.

- Develop a national integrated plan for ICT support to Open Government.

- Examine opportunities to consolidate and streamline existing websites.

- Develop alternative Open Government mechanisms and communication strategies to reach citizens lacking access to online services.

- Expand the use of social media to communicate with citizens, including development of smartphone applications.

Source: OECD, 2016b

Despite the considerable progress made through the adoption of new laws, new mechanisms for participation and transparency, Tunisia still faces significant challenges in streamlining open government principles and practices within the administration and society. This report highlights opportunities and challenges at the local level, specifically in the municipalities of La Marsa, Sayada and Sfax.

National government initiatives for open government and their impact on municipalities

The national government of Tunisia has made a commitment to open government, enshrining these principles in its legal framework, and it has demonstrated its commitment at the international level by joining the OGP. In this context, the government has launched a multitude of reforms to promote transparency, participation and accountability. These reforms include commitments made as part of open government action plans, but they also go beyond these, for example in terms of budget transparency, open data (through a national portal) and the fight against corruption (through the adoption of a Code of Conduct for Public Officials). Several of these commitments have an impact on open government at the local level. In addition, recognising the importance of local authorities being more open and closer to the citizens, the government itself has made more concrete commitments to encourage open government at the local level through the second OGP action plan, which states that:

- The Ministry of Local Affairs and the Environment has pledged to develop a practical guide to explain the principles of open government and set up open data platforms at the municipal level.

- The Ministry of Youth and Sports has undertaken to set up youth consultative councils at the local level.

These commitments represent a first step towards addressing the difficulties encountered in the area of local citizen participation, especially for youth. Their effective and full implementation could help overcome a number of shortcomings and meet various challenges in establishing local open government practices, particularly at the municipal level, in terms of expertise in youth participation and transparency. However, to better target and harness the national open government programme as an engine of development for the whole country, structures for involving local administrations in national projects should be considered, such as involving local administrations in the Steering Committee for Open Government or in open data initiatives.

In addition, the Urban Development and Local Government Programme (PDUGL), launched in 2015 and described below, has a direct impact on open government at the local level, since it stipulates open government practices as a condition for the awarding of subsidies to local authorities. PDUGL is a 1.220 million dinar (about 418 million euro) programme, partly funded by a World Bank loan over a period of 60 months, which aims to implement the principles of decentralisation laid out in the Constitution.

A new system of transferring subsidies to municipalities has been developed on the basis of a transparency performance assessment and the respect of mandatory minimum conditions. The municipalities are required to prepare and adopt a Municipal Investment Plan (MIP) for the next five years. According to a circular dated 14 August 2013 from the Ministry of the Interior, the principles to be respected in preparing the MIP include the adoption of a participatory approach, transparency and good local governance, as well as the effective and efficient use of local authority resources. A participatory approach is also required for preparation of the Annual Investment Plan (AIP). The programme's executing agency is the Loans and Support Fund for Local Authorities (CPSCL). A precise timetable and a public consultation guide by the CPSCL give a detailed outline of the steps for municipalities to follow in developing their AIP/MIP, including an annual public meeting to provide information on municipal activities and to allow citizens to voice their opinions on the AIP/MIP (see Figure 1.2).

Figure 1.2. Involvement of the public in the PDUGL framework

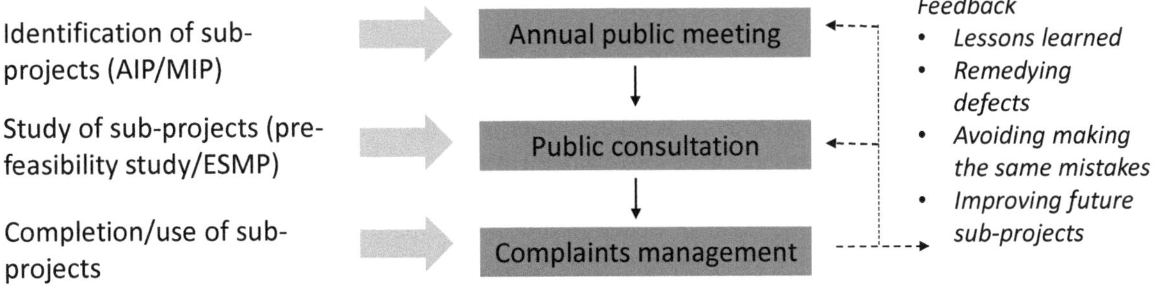

Source: CPSCL, 2015.

The municipalities were required to prepare their first AIP in 2016. While the introduction of a participatory approach in all municipalities through the AIP/MIP is a commendable reform for the promotion of open government, the AIP has been introduced at a time when several municipalities had already independently developed a participatory approach, also to participatory budgeting. Under the current arrangements, the AIP mechanism does not take these mechanisms into account, which has created confusion and generated parallel mechanisms in municipalities that have already adopted participatory budgeting (see below for a detailed discussion on this point).

In addition, in an effort to establish transparency, within the framework of the PDUGL, the Ministry of Local Affairs and the Environment launched a local authorities' portal (www.collectiviteslocales.gov.tn). The aim of the portal is to "entrench the concepts of transparency, good governance and participation in the authorities"[4]. The portal provides data on finances (budgets) and performance (governance, management, sustainability) for each municipality, including in open data format. It also offers information linked to the PDGUL, as well as to the legal and regulatory framework. A space for e-complaints allows citizens to register their grievances.

To strengthen national programmes, such as the PDUGL, which aims to implement open government practices at the local level, it would be useful to involve local administrations to a greater extent and to build on the processes and mechanisms developed at the local level. Closer involvement of local administrations, for example through representative institutions (the future High Council of Local Authorities as well as the National Federation of Tunisian Cities), will help programmes adapt better to local needs and conditions, and will encourage political commitment on the part of local actors. Several OECD countries have developed mechanisms for involving subnational governments (see Box 1.2).

Box 1.2. Consultation of subnational governments on open government: case studies from Spain and Peru

In Spain, consultations were initially conducted through the National Commission for Local Administrations (CNAL), the standing body for collaboration between the central government and local governments. With the adoption of the 3rd National OGP Action Plan, the Sectorial Commission on Open Government was launched on 6 March 2017 and is made up of the General State Administration and the Autonomous Communities, Autonomous Cities and the Spanish Federation of Municipalities and Provinces (FEMP). It serves as an organ of inter-administrative cooperation and a forum for exchanging information among the three levels of public administration.

In Peru, the three levels of government, namely the ministries, the regional administrations and the municipalities, have been involved in developing the National OGP Action Plan 2015-2016. The Ministry of Public Management requested these to propose their commitments for the action plan. In addition, participatory workshops have been organised in the departments of Ayacucho, Piura, San Martín and Lima, with the aim of identifying proposals for commitments, thereby shaping a joint vision between the regions and municipalities.

Sources: OECD, 2017b; Spanish Ministry of Finance and Civil Service (Ministerio de Hacienda y Función Pública)
http://transparencia.gob.es/transparencia/transparencia_Home/index/GobiernoParticipacion/Gobierno-abierto/IIIPlan.html; http://transparencia.gob.es/transparencia/dam/jcr:cfc2ac4b-a5bb-4fc2-857d-4fbf61864122/2017_07_26_SPA-ENG_III_Plan_OGP_vf-1.pdf.

References

CPSCL (2015), Guide sur la consultation publique pour les collectivités locales, http://www.collectiviteslocales.gov.tn/wp-content/uploads/2015/06/GUIDE-de-la-consultation-publique.pdf (accessed on 29 January 2018).

GIZ (2014), La démocratie locale et la participation des citoyens à l'action municipale: Tunisie.

Ministère des Affaires Locales et de l'Environnement (2017), Portail des Collectivités Locales en Tunisie, http://www.collectiviteslocales.gov.tn/ (accessed on 29 January 2018).

OECD (2017a), Recommendation of the Council on Open Government http://acts.oecd.org (accessed on 29 January 2018).

OECD (2017b), *Towards a New Partnership with Citizens - Jordan's Decentralisation Reform*, OECD Publishing.

OECD (2016a) Open Government: The Global Context and the Way Forward, OECD Publishing, Paris, https://doi.org/10.1787/9789264268104-en

OECD (2016b) Open Government in Tunisia, OECD Publishing, Paris, https://doi.org/10.1787/9789264227118-en

Notes

[1] Examples include the engagement of civil society for the adoption of a law on the right to access to information, in line with international standards, or citizens' protests against a new law on security, which they see as an attack on freedom of expression (www.hrw.org/news/2015/05/13/tunisia-drop-or-amend-security-bill).

[2] For more details, see OECD, Open Government in Tunisia (2016).

[3] For more information on the process in Tunisia, see: www.ogptunisie.gov.tn/.

[4] Presentation of the portal.

Chapter 2. Open government and decentralisation

This chapter explores key aspects of the planned decentralisation process and analyses the impact of this transition on the functioning of local administration and on open government at the local level. The experience of other OECD countries forms the basis of recommendations that can help to create an enabling environment to ensure that decentralisation and open government can lead to better local development.

Territorial organisation and the role of local authorities in Tunisia

Tunisia is a unitary state whose highly centralised character dates back to pre-colonial and colonial times, a choice that was maintained after independence. The Constitution of 1959 only devoted one article (Article 71 of Chapter VIII) to local authorities, which stipulated that "municipal councils, regional councils and structures to which the law confers the quality of local government manage local affairs in the conditions provided for by law". Territorial organisation was based on a logic of devolution, with land divided up into governorates, delegations and sectors, and one of decentralisation, with regional councils, municipalities, districts (*arrondissements*) and areas without municipal organisation (Turki and Verdeil, 2015) (see Figure 2.1).

The municipalities are governed by a mayor who is elected at municipal elections. When the logic of devolution prevailed (see Box 2.1), there was an absence of real, local democracy (EU Committee of the Regions, 2014). The prerogatives and competences of the municipal authority were limited and restricted, and the municipalities' work was framed by the governors, the regional directorates of ministerial departments and national agencies (OECD, 2017a). These limitations, which were compounded by a lack of resources and expertise, resulted in the inability of municipalities to develop real public policies in the key areas of urban and land planning. This hampered their ability to plan the development of their municipalities, promote development projects, and provide quality public services. Furthermore, the manner in which the elections were held, with the dominance of the party in power, contributed to municipal councils being insufficiently representative. Finally, the absence of communication between the municipality and citizens did not allow for good relations to grow between the two. As a result, even today, the municipalities are faced with a refusal by citizens to pay local taxes and citizens' non-compliance with urban and environmental regulations (Turki and Verdeil, 2015).

Box 2.1. Devolution and decentralisation

Decentralisation: "Decentralisation consists of transferring competences from the State to institutions that are distinct from it, also known as local authorities. These latter enjoy autonomy of decision-making and have their own finances, to a greater or lesser extent depending on the country" (OECD, 2017a). A distinction can be made between political decentralisation (transfer of political power), fiscal/budgetary decentralisation (reallocation of financial resources) and administrative decentralisation (transfer of decision-making power and responsibility for the provision of public services) (OECD, 2017b).

Devolution: "Administrative devolution consists of delegating the powers of the State to local agents or bodies that remain subject to the authority of the State and only enjoy limited autonomy" (OECD, 2017b).

The decentralisation (see Box 2.1) provided for in Chapter 7 of the 2014 Constitution represents a response to this lack of local democracy and municipalities' limited capacity to take charge of their own development. To address these shortcomings, Tunisia chose to enshrine in its Constitution concepts such as local power, decentralisation, local interests, self-government, financial and administrative autonomy, the principle of subsidiarity, the election of councils and the autonomy of competences (EU Committee of the Regions, 2014) (OECD, 2017a). The Constitution lays out three categories of local authorities, namely municipalities, regions and districts. In this way, it creates a new territorial organisation, adding districts (see Figure 2.1). A district (*iklim*) consists of more than one governorate and is managed by a district council elected by members of local authorities. However, the division of districts has not yet been decided (EU Committee of the Regions, 2014). In addition, the municipalities have witnessed a development with the creation of 25 new municipalities in 2015 and 61 new municipalities in 2016, increasing the total number from 264 to 350. Following a constitutional provision, Government Decree No. 2016-602 dated 26 May 2016 completes the full coverage of Tunisian territory in terms of municipal administration, whereas previously, some 3.5 million Tunisians, mainly in rural regions, had lived without municipal representation. The division of governorates and delegations has not, however, been affected by these changes (Drugeon, 2016).

Figure 2.1. Territorial organisation in Tunisia before the new Constitution and since 2016

Before 2011 and since 2016

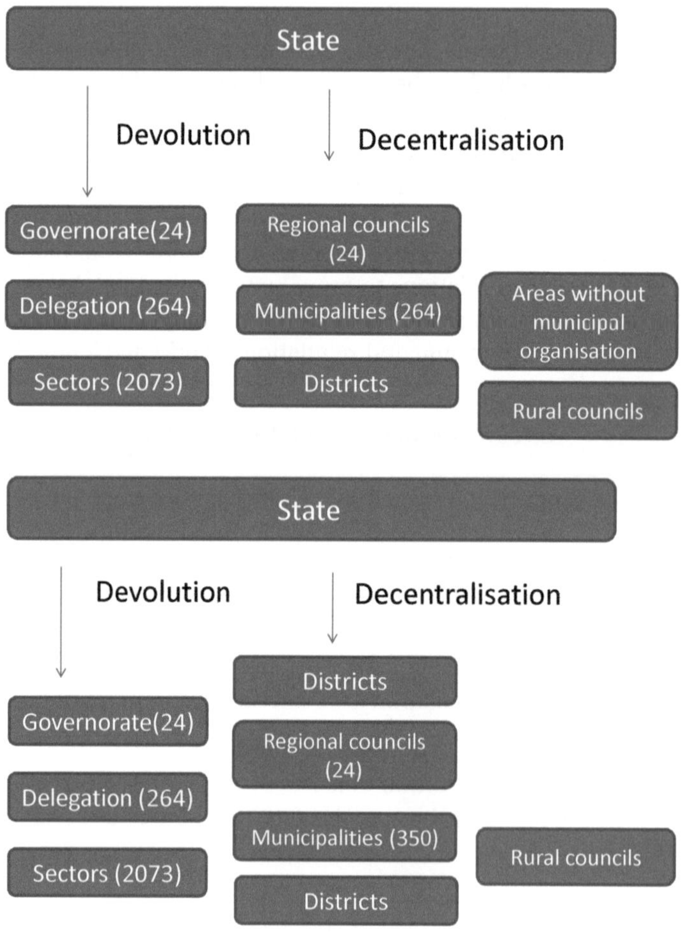

Source: Turki and Verdeil, 2015, and author.

The municipalities were managed by special delegations up until the elections of May 2018. The municipal councils were dissolved after the 2011 revolution and replaced by special delegations, appointed in accordance with the organic law on municipalities[1]. Although these special delegations were initially appointed for one year, they are still in place – some municipalities have seen the appointment of new delegations – and remained in operation for more than seven years until the municipal elections.

Progress in the decentralisation process

Tunisia is currently in a transition phase with, on the one hand, a new Constitution that establishes the principles of local power and, on the other, local authorities that operate under former laws drafted under the regime of Ben Ali, pending the implementation of the newly approved Law on Local Authorities.

Chapter VII of the 2014 Constitution sets out the principles of local power. It stipulates, among other things, that:

- Local government is based on decentralisation (Article 131).

- Local authorities shall enjoy legal personality as well as financial and administrative independence. They manage local matters in accordance with the principle of administrative autonomy (Article 132).

- Local authorities possess their own powers, powers shared with the central authority, and powers delegated to them from the central government. The joint and delegated powers shall be distributed in accordance with the principle of subsidiarity. Local authorities shall enjoy regulatory powers in exercising their mandates. Regulatory decisions of the local authorities shall be published in an official gazette of local authorities (Article 134).

- Local authorities shall have their own resources, and resources provided to them by the central government, these resources being proportional to the responsibilities that are assigned to them by law (Article 135).

- Local authorities shall adopt the mechanisms of participatory democracy and the principles of open governance to ensure the broadest participation of citizens and of civil society in the preparation of development programmes and land use planning, and follow up on their implementation, in conformity with the law (Article 139).

- Local authorities may cooperate and enter into partnerships with each other with a view to implementing programmes or carrying out activities of common interest. Local authorities may also establish foreign relations of partnership and decentralised cooperation (Article 140).

Chapter VII marks a break with the old Constitution, which stipulated that local authorities should exclusively manage local affairs. The new Constitution strengthens the role of local authorities and guarantees them greater powers than the old one, among which the principle of self-government should be highlighted.

To implement decentralisation and the principles laid out by the Constitution in a progressive manner, a Code for Local Authorities was adopted by Parliament on 27 April 2018; however, the new competences will only be transferred gradually to the municipalities, over a period of nine years (Drugeon, 2016).

At the same time, progress was made regarding long-awaited local elections, the timing of which had been postponed several times. The adoption by the Assembly of People's Representatives of Organic Law No. 2017-7 on 14 February 2017, amending and supplementing Organic Law No. 2014-16 of 26 May 2014 on the elections, and the referendums of 31 January 2017 (AFP, 2017) paved the way for this ballot, which should embed the democratic process at the local level. However, the resignation on 9 May 2017 of the President of Tunisia's Independent High Authority for Elections, together with several other members of the authority due to internal tensions linked to democratic principles (Bellamine, 2017a), triggered a debate on the date for the elections, which were postponed (RFI, 2017) (Bellamine, 2017b) and then finally held on 6 May 2018.

Pending implementation of the Code for Local Authorities and during the past seven years, the municipalities have and continue to be regulated by the 1975 organic law on municipalities (Law No. 75-33 of 14 May 1975 promulgating the organic law on municipalities amended in 2008 by Law No. 2008-57 of 4 August 2008). According to Article 21, the competences of municipalities are as follows.

Through debate, the municipal council manages the affairs of the municipality:

- It examines and approves the municipal budget.

- Within the constraints of the municipality's resources and the means made available to it, it decides the local authority's investment programme.

- Decisions are made in line with the national development plan for the area.

- It gives its opinion on all matters of local interest, particularly on economic, social and cultural issues, and at all times when this opinion is regulated by laws and regulations, or is required by the supervisory authority.

- It convenes in advance for all projects to be carried out by the State or any other public authority or body on the municipal territory.

In addition, the municipality is responsible for developing, implementing and monitoring the development plan (Article 119). The municipality's principal prerogatives are listed in Article 118, which sets out the traditional competences of basic public services in the area of road maintenance and municipal works, including the development of urban roads, gardens and green spaces, lighting, waste treatment, cleaning of public places, and the maintenance of municipal buildings. At first glance, few competences are given to municipalities in the area of strategic planning. The spirit of the new Constitution reflects a fresh approach that assigns a more prominent role to municipalities in the field of municipal management. Box 2.2 shows the competences of subnational governments in the OECD countries.

Box 2.2. The system of sub-national administrations and their competencies in OECD countries

Number of sub-national administrations

		Municipal level	Intermediary level	Regional or state level	Total
Federations and quasi- federations	Australia	563		8	571
	Austria	2122		9	2131
	Belgium	589	10	6	605
	Canada	3945		13	3958
	Germany	11056	401	16	11473
	Mexico	2458		32	2490
	Spain	8125	50	17	8192
	Switzerland	2255		26	2281
	United States	35879	3031	50	38960
Unitary countries	Chile	345		15	360
	Czech Republic	6256		14	6270
	Denmark	98		5	103
	Estonia	213			213
	Finland	311		1	312
	France	35416	101	18	35535
	Greece	325		13	338
	Hungary	3178		19	3197
	Iceland	74			74
	Ireland	31			31
	Israel	255			255
	Italy	7982		20	8002
	Japan	1742		47	1789
	Korea	227		17	244
	Latvia	119			119
	Luxembourg	105			105
	Netherlands	388		12	400
	New Zealand	67		11	78
	Norway	426		18	444
	Poland	2478	380	16	2874
	Portugal	308		2	310
	Slovak Republic	2929		8	2937
	Slovenia	212			212
	Sweden	290		21	311
	Turkey	1397		81	1478
	United Kingdom	391	27	3	421
OECD-35		132555	4000	518	137073
MENA	Jordan	94	12		112
	Morocco	1538	75	12	1625
	Tunisia	350	24		

Responsibilities across different levels of government

Municipal level	Intermediary level	Regional level
Services for the municipalities: • Education (nursery schools, pre-elementary and primary education) • Urban planning and management • Local utility networks (water, sewerage, waste, hygiene, etc.) • Local roads and city public transport • Social affairs (support for families and children, elderly, disabled, poverty, social benefits, etc.) • Primary and preventative healthcare • Recreation (sport) and culture • Public order and safety (municipal police, fire brigades) • Local economic development, tourism, trade fairs • Environment (green areas) • Social housing • Administrative and permit services	Specialised and more limited responsibilities of supra-municipal interest An important role of assistance towards small municipalities May exercise responsibilities delegated by the regions and central government Responsibilities determined by functional level and the geographic area • Secondary education and specialised education • Supra-municipal social and youth welfare • Waste treatment • Secondary roads and public transport • Environment	Heterogeneous and more or less extensive responsibilities depending on countries (in particular, federal vs. unitary) Services of regional interest: • Secondary/higher education and professional training • Spatial planning • Regional economic development and innovation • Health (secondary care and hospitals) • Social affairs e.g. employment services, training, inclusion, support to special groups, etc. • Regional roads and public transport • Culture, heritage and tourism • Environmental protection • Social housing • Public order and safety (e.g. regional police, civil protection) • Local government supervision (in federal countries)

Note: The statistical data for Israel are supplied by and under the responsibility of the relevant Israeli authorities. The use of such data by the OECD is without prejudice to the status of the Golan Heights, East Jerusalem and Israeli settlements in the West Bank under the terms of international law. Includes only subnational government with general competencies. **Netherlands: 403 municipalities as of 1 January 2014. *** The regional level in Portugal includes only two overseas regions: Madeira and Azores.

Sources: OECD, *Subnational governments in OECD countries: Key data* (2016) (brochure); OECD, *Regions at a Glance 2016*, OECD Publishing, Paris (2016), Decree No. 2.15.40 of 20 February 2015 (Morocco), and www.hcp.ma/Repartition-geographique-de-la-population-d-apres-les-donnees-du-Recensement-General-de-la-Population-et-de-l-Habitat-de_a1796.html.

According to the Code for Local Authorities, municipalities' competences will be extended by adding their own competences, those shared with the central government, and competences transferred to them by the latter. The competences will be distributed according to the principle of subsidiarity. The transfer of competences must be accompanied by a proportional transfer of funds and resources. Own competences include the supply of local services and amenities. In addition, the municipal council is responsible for managing the affairs of the municipality, including its financial commitments, and for setting taxes. It is charged with drawing up the investment and equipment programme and the urban development plan. The shared competences include tasks such as developing the local economy, while transferred competences focus on the construction and renovation of certain public facilities. In addition, local authorities have regulatory power. This involves a decentralisation that extends past a simple devolution (IACE, 2015).

The current context places municipalities in a complex situation. They must find a balance between, on the one hand, the demands of citizens and the new competences that they should receive, and, on the other, the tutelage of old laws. This situation generates a lack of legitimacy linked to inadequate capacities and to the appointment of special delegations, which had managed the municipalities until the local elections were held. Furthermore, since the revolution, municipalities have lost their authority over the municipal police, which has deprived them of an executive power and further reduced their scope for manoeuvring in response to citizens' needs, and especially in halting the various violations of municipal regulations, such as unauthorised constructions or illegal land occupancy by cafés, businesses and restaurants. Since 2011, the police has been placed under the authority of the district chief of security (Ministry of Interior), while the municipality retains responsibility for providing the logistical support necessary for the performance of its duties. The fact that municipalities no longer have authority over the police, coupled with the assignment of police to other tasks, creates a situation that is difficult for municipalities to manage (Lajili, 2016). Once the decentralisation policy is set in place, the municipalities should regain authority in this area.

While the reforms for decentralisation are slow to come about, the municipalities also face structural problems that they have difficulty in addressing. Tunisia has experienced a wave of strikes in the urban service sector, which have resulted in tenure being granted to contract staff, and an ensuing increase in the total wage bill. Furthermore, municipal resources have fallen following a decline in payments of local taxes. For example, in 2011, municipalities suffered a 37% decline in their own resources and, in certain municipalities, the wage burden exceeds their revenues (Turki and Verdeil, 2015). Regional disparities persist, although the share of the state budget allocated to regional development has more than quadrupled since 2011 (Ben Raies, 2015). Against this backdrop, the special delegations, which lacked democratic legitimacy since they were not elected, have responded to citizens demanding the right to participation by trying to become more open and by experimenting with new forms of interaction with communities. In addition, pending the adoption of the Code for Local Authorities and the holding of municipal elections, the central government has implemented programmes and initiatives for regional development, namely the Urban Development and Local Government Programme described in the first chapter, which imposes requirements and conditions on the municipalities, in terms of implementing a participatory process. This situation has an impact on their open government initiatives, particularly on participatory budgeting as discussed in greater detail below. Tunisia is still today in a transitional stage of defining its model of open government at the local level, with citizen participation at its centre. On this point, the principles of the Council of Europe could serve as a source of inspiration (see Box 2.3).

Box 2.3. The 12 principles of good democratic governance at the local level

In 2008, the member states of the Council of Europe approved principles of good democratic governance to be promoted at the local level. They recognised, however, that "a necessary precondition for the implementation of these Principles is that local authorities have the powers, responsibilities and resources enabling them to regulate and manage a substantial share of public affairs under their own responsibility and in the interest of the local population".

These principles are:

1. Fair Conduct of Elections, Representation and Participation, to ensure real possibilities for all citizens to have their say in local public affairs.

2. Responsiveness, to ensure that the local authority meets the legitimate expectations and needs of citizens.

3. Efficiency and Effectiveness, to ensure that objectives are met while making the best use of resources.

4. Openness and Transparency, to ensure public access to information and facilitate understanding of how local public affairs are conducted.

5. Rule of Law, to ensure fairness, impartiality and predictability.

6. Ethical Conduct, to ensure that the public interest is put before private ones.

7. Competence and Capacity, to ensure that local representatives and officials are well able to carry out their duties.

8. Innovation and Openness to Change, to ensure that benefit is derived from new solutions and good practices.

9. Sustainability and Long-term Orientation, to take the interests of future generations into account.

10. Sound Financial Management, to ensure prudent and productive use of public funds.

11. Human rights, Cultural Diversity and Social Cohesion, to ensure that all citizens are protected and respected and that no one is either discriminated against or excluded.

12. Accountability, to ensure that local representatives and officials take responsibility and are held responsible for their actions.

Source: Council of Europe, 2007.

However, establishing and implementing decentralisation remains a key ingredient for the success of open government at the local level. Certainty regarding competences and resources would enable local administrations to develop long-term approaches, and thereby help to build trust among citizens. Social movements that have developed in recent years, particularly in the most marginalised regions, attest to the importance of implementing a decentralisation reform that responds to citizens' needs. That requires inter-ministerial coordination, including between the Ministry of Local Affairs and Environment, the Ministry of Finance, and especially the unit responsible for open government within the

Presidency of the Government. Such coordination would ensure the alignment between the local development and decentralisation policies, and human and financial resources.

References

AFP (2017), "L'Assemblée vote la loi relative aux élections et aux référendums, les élections municipales en point de mire", HuffPost Tunisie, http://www.huffpostmaghreb.com/2017/01/31/loi-elections-municipales_n_14524362.html (accessed on 29 January 2018).

Bellamine, Y. (2017a), "Face aux députés: Chafik Sarsar craint que l'ISIE ne puisse plus garantir des élections démocratiques", HuffPost Tunisie, http://www.huffpostmaghreb.com/2017/05/10/chafik-sarsar-assemblee_n_16537870.html (accessed on 29 January 2018).

Bellamine, Y. (2017b), "Démission de Chafik Sarsar: Quel avenir pour les élections municipales?", HuffPost Tunisie, http://www.huffpostmaghreb.com/2017/05/09/elections-municipales-tun_n_16509074.html (accessed on 29 January 2018).

Ben Raies, M. (2015), "De la décentralisation en question, Quelle Tunisie ?", Leaders, http://www.leaders.com.tn/article/17501-de-la-decentralisation-en-question-quelle-tunisie (accessed on 29 January 2018).

Council of Europe (2007), Extrait de la Déclaration de de Valencia de la 15e Conférence des Ministres européens responsables des collectivités locales et régionales, https://rm.coe.int/168070169a%20et%20www.coe.int/fr/web/good-governance/12-principles-and-eloge (accessed on 29 January 2018).

Drugeon, A. (2016), "La Tunisie en passe de créer 61 nouvelles municipalités", HuffPost Tunisie, http://www.huffpostmaghreb.com/2016/05/26/tunisie-61-municipalites_n_10140830.html (accessed on 29 January 2018).

European Committee of the Regions (2014), Tunisie: Fiche Technique - Répartition verticale des compétences, https://portal.cor.europa.eu/arlem/Documents/Tunisia%20Fact%20Sheet%20No%201%20FR%20_%208%20May%202014.pdf (accessed on 29 January 2018).

IACE (2015), Guide de Bonnes Pratiques de Gouvernance Locale, http://www.iace.tn/wp-content/uploads/2017/02/Guide_gouvernance-locale_version-finale.pdf (accessed on 29 January 2018).

Lajili, T. (2016), "Tunisie: Police municipale - Un statut ambigu - allAfrica.com", La Presse.tn, http://fr.allafrica.com/stories/201610210888.html (accessed on 29 January 2018).

OECD (2017a), Un meilleur contrôle pour une meilleure gouvernance locale en Tunisie : Le contrôle des finances publiques au niveau local, Examens de l'OCDE sur la gouvernance publique, OECD Publishing, Paris, http://dx.doi.org/10.1787/9789264265967-fr.

OECD (2017b), *Towards a New Partnership with Citizens - Jordan's Decentralisation Reform*, OECD Publishing.

RFI (2017), *Tunisie: des ONG dénoncent le report des élections municipales - RFI*, RFI, www.rfi.fr/afrique/20170919-tunisie-ong-denoncent-le-report-elections-municipales (accessed 29 January 2018).

Turki, S. and Verdeil, E. (2015), "Tunisie: la Constitution (du Printemps) Ouvre le Débat sur la Décentralisation", dans *Local Governments and Public Goods: Assessing Decentralization in the Arab World*, LCPS, https://halshs.archives-ouvertes.fr/halshs-01221381/document (accessed 29 January 2018).

Notes

[1] In the event that a municipal council be dissolved, or all its incumbent members resign, or it is impossible to form a municipal council, a special delegation will take over these duties. [...] This delegation is appointed by decree. [...] This special delegation and its president perform the same duties as the municipal council and its president." Article 12, Law No. 75-33 of 14 May 1975, promulgating the organic law on municipalities.

Chapter 3. Open Government in La Marsa, Sayada and Sfax

This chapter offers an assessment of the institutional framework and open government practices in the municipalities of La Marsa, Sayada and Sfax. It provides an overview of current practices and their opportunities and weaknesses in the context of the open government principles enshrined in the Code for Local Authorities. Recommendations for a more consistent and systematic approach are developed based on the experience of the OECD countries and the OECD Recommendation on Open Government.

The special delegations of municipalities appointed in 2011 have been faced with citizen expectations for more inclusive and open public governance that is capable of overcoming the challenges of local development. In this context, a number of mayors and municipal councillors have taken the initiative to implement practices that create a more open and citizen-centred local administration. The legitimacy deficit arising from the absence of elections increased the urgency and importance of including citizens in the management of public policies and municipal services. This culture of openness sought to break with the culture of secrecy and establish a climate of trust. The new mechanisms for participation and transparency, especially in the area of finance, had the additional goal of fostering citizens' interest in municipal affairs and restoring confidence in municipal management, also to encourage them to pay their local taxes (Guidara, 2015).

Citizens and civil society did not wait for a new system of governance to be put in place, and instead came forward as drivers of change, proposing new forms of citizen participation to the municipalities. The engagement on the part of civil society, coupled with the new spirit of openness shown by the municipalities, have led to the introduction of promising open government practices in some municipalities, namely participatory budgeting and open data initiatives. The municipalities of La Marsa, Sayada and Sfax are part of these innovative experiences. La Marsa and Sfax are among the few municipalities to have adopted participatory budgeting, and Sayada has set-up a partnership with civil society in an effort to make the municipality more transparent.

In light of these experiences and the commitment of the national government to promote open government principles and initiatives, the open government team in Tunisia, together with the Ministry of Local Affairs and Environment, has chosen the municipalities of La Marsa, Sayada and Sfax for cooperation and a pilot study with the OECD. The aim of this cooperation is to review the legal and institutional policy frameworks, as well as open government practices in the three pilot municipalities, to increase their importance and impact on the one hand, and to share their best practices and lessons learned with all Tunisian municipalities on the other.

Characteristics of La Marsa, Sayada and Sfax

La Marsa, Sayada and Sfax are coastal municipalities in the north and centre of Tunisia. They are located in the governorates of Tunis (La Marsa), Monastir (Sayada) and Sfax (Municipality of Sfax). These municipalities are situated in the country's most developed governorates. Tunis and Sfax hold first and second place in the local business climate index, and Monastir lies in eighth place. The index assesses municipal services, the participatory approach, transparency and access to information, non-municipal services, living conditions and the availability of labour (IACE, 2016). These governorates also host important economic sectors for Tunisia, namely agriculture, textiles, leather, fisheries and the chemical industry.

The Regional Development Index (2012) also shows that Tunis, in 1st place with a score of 0.76. Monastir, in 4th position with 0.64, and Sfax, in 7th place with 0.56, rank among the country's top 7 regions, compared with more marginalised regions such as Kairouan (23rd place, with 0.25) or Kasserine (24th place, with 0.16). It is important to note the significant differences between Tunis (0.76) and Kasserine (0.16)[1].

In terms of social and economic indicators (see Table 3.1), the three municipalities show results that are above average for Tunisia, particularly regarding unemployment and levels of education or Internet connectivity. Compared with other municipalities, this positions them at an advantage for piloting and implementing new open government practices.

Table 3.1. General Census of Population and Housing 2014

	La Marsa	Sfax	Sayada- Lamta- Bouhjar	Tunisia
Population	92 987	272 801	24 889 12 962 (Sayada)	10 982 754
Youth (15-29)	23.7%	23.8%	26.5%	25%
Illiterate (10+)	9.3%	12%	10.9%	18.8%
Use of Internet (10+)	57.9%	47%	46.9%	36.9% (total area) 45,4% (municipal area)
Unemployment	9%	9%	7.2%	14.8%
Unemployment (men)	7.3%	6.2%	4.8%	11.4%
Unemployment (women)	11.8%	14.3%	10.5%	22.2%

Note: The figures for Sfax except for the population refer to the Sfax city delegation.
Source: INS, 2014, General Census of Population and Housing 2014.

Towards a comprehensive approach to open government at the local level

OECD data shows that despite the existence of a great many open government practices at the level of national and subnational governments, a consistent approach often remains lacking, even though this is important for a cultural change to occur, and for strategic use to be made of open government. As a result, the OECD Recommendation on Open Government proposes that adherents "develop, adopt and implement open government strategies and initiatives". According to the recommendation's definition, "an open government strategy (is) a document that defines the open government agenda of the central government and/or of any of its sub-national levels, as well as that of a single public institution or thematic area, and that includes key open government initiatives, together with short, medium and long-term goals and indicators" (OECD, 2017a).

In Tunisia, in terms of the central government, the biennial open government action plans are more of a roadmap for open government than an actual strategy. Municipalities, including La Marsa, Sayada and Sfax, have developed open government practices (which are discussed below) that are, however, not part of a strategic vision. For this reason, the municipalities could develop their own open government strategy at the local level, as in the case of the region of North Rhine-Westphalia in Germany (see Box 3.1). The mayors and elected representatives could, in consultation with citizens, reach a consensus on key priorities in the areas of transparency, stakeholder participation, integrity and accountability, taking inspiration from the new prerogatives in the Code for Local Authorities. Such a strategy would include the vision, objectives and activities to be undertaken, as well as a calendar and indicators for an impact assessment.

An open government strategy would enable a long-term approach to be taken, beyond the elections, and ensure consistency between all the activities, while bringing all the stakeholders together around the same vision. It would also help to align the activities more closely with the human and financial resources available, and to draw up a roadmap to develop these resources. Strategies could be developed for each municipality. Nevertheless, exchanges could be useful in harmonising these strategies, so that municipalities could learn from each other and adopt a joint approach towards the central government.

Box 3.1. Open Government strategy of the federal state of North Rhine-Westphalia (NRW) in Germany

Developing this strategy was among the commitments made in the 2012-2017 government coalition agreement, with the aim of developing a new culture of participation in the digital age and strengthening transparency in the administration. With this objective, the strategy was adopted in 2014. It presents a consistent and ambitious approach with a practical focus. The strategy is based on the principles of participation, transparency and collaboration.

Key points of the strategy are:

- An inter-ministerial approach that seeks to involve the entire administration.

- An integrated approach that includes participation, transparency and collaboration.

- A participatory approach to developing the strategy.

The key objectives are to:

- Strengthen dialogue between citizens and the administration to build greater trust.

- Open up administrative action to citizens, the private sector and universities to give it fresh impetus.

- Draw on the potential for innovation in open government.

Activities within the strategy include:

- Creation of the necessary institutional framework within the administration.

- Open data.

- Participation through online standards and mechanisms.

- e-collaboration, in-house and with civil society.

- The Open.NRW portal as a central platform for open government.

- Internal and external communication about Open.NRW.

- Information, training and cultural change in the administration.

- Assessment of strategy implementation.

Source: The state government of North Rhine-Westphalia, 2014.

The institutional framework for open government in La Marsa, Sayada and Sfax

The successful implementation of open government practices and the development of a strategy in this area also depend on the administration's institutional framework. Analyses conducted in the OECD countries have shown the value of dedicated structures for coordinating open government initiatives to ensure their consistency, complementarity and relevance. Some 77% of OECD countries have a service responsible for the horizontal coordination of open government initiatives at the central level. The study shows that this service is responsible for a number of tasks linked to the implementation of open government reforms, such as: formulating an open government strategy, coordinating the implementation, monitoring and evaluation of open government initiatives, communication and, in some cases, allocating financial resources and evaluating the impact (see Figure 3.1) (OECD, 2016a).

Figure 3.1. Responsibilities of the coordination office

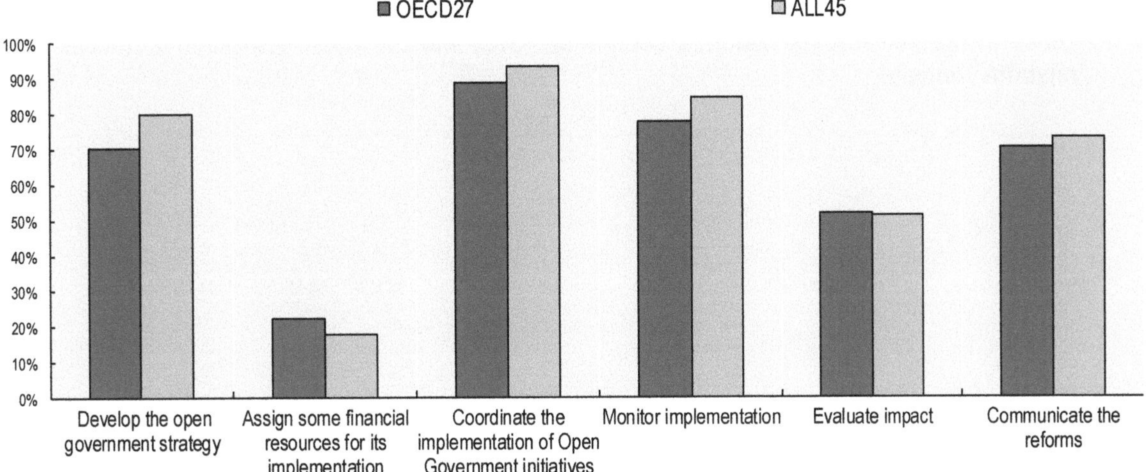

Source: OECD (2016a).

Following the 2011 revolution and dissolution of the municipal councils, special delegations were appointed by decree in all the country's municipalities. This process also applied to the cities of La Marsa, Sayada and Sfax, enabling them to manage municipal activities until local elections were held in accordance with Article 12 of the organic law on municipalities. However, all three municipalities experienced several delegation changes, meaning that each one had to re-establish a dialogue with the citizens, while the local community was forced to remind the new delegations of the open government commitments made by the outgoing ones. These changes had an impact on the initiatives, particularly in Sayada[2]. This municipality found itself in an unusual situation following the resignation of the president and members of the special delegation on 26 October 2015 (Businessnews, 2015); as a result, it was led by the Governor of Monastir for more than a year, until a new delegation was nominated on 8 February 2017[3]. The special delegation in La Marsa was replaced just two months (9 June 2011[4]) after its initial nomination (8 April 2011[5]) as a result of dissatisfaction among local actors, according to explanations from the leaders of La Marsa. Sfax saw the nomination of a new delegation in October 2012[6]. Finally, the compositions of delegations in La Marsa and Sfax were changed in April 2017[7]. The municipal councils elected during the local elections of May 2018 are now being called on to continue the dialogue with citizens to win their trust.

The special delegations of the past seven years have been headed by the mayor and are made up of several members. The fact that they remained in place for longer than the one-year period initially planned resulted in some members becoming inactive. Delegation members were responsible for the municipality's eight permanent committees, which handle administrative and financial affairs, urban works and planning, health, sanitation and environmental protection, economic, social, family, youth, sports and cultural affairs, co-operation and external relations, and voluntary action (law of 1975). By contrast, in Sayada, two committees had to be merged, due to the limited number of delegation members.

The municipal administration has a similar structure in all three municipalities and consists of several departments (see Figure 3.2 for La Marsa, Figure 3.3 for Sfax and Figure 3.4 for Sayada). The appointment of an official with responsibility for access to information in each administration is obligatory under Article 32 of the organic law on the right to access to information, while the appointment of an official with responsibility for handling complaints is a requirement of the PDUGL programme, with the role clearly defined in the Guide to mechanisms for handling complaints. Sfax and La Marsa also have a citizens' relations' bureau.

Figure 3.2. Administrative structure of the municipality of La Marsa

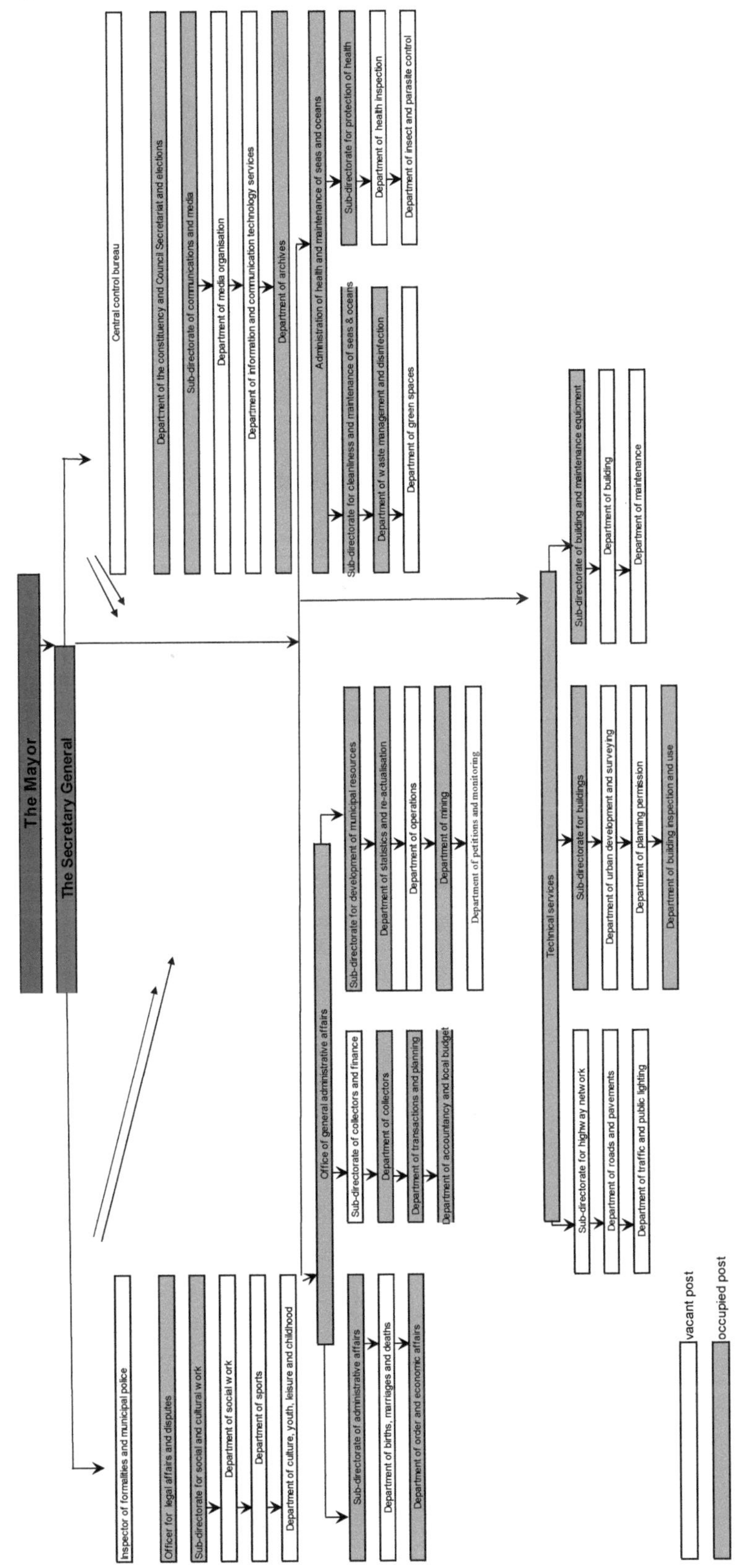

Source: La Marsa, 2017, www.communemarsa.tn/services-de-la-commune/?lang=ar.

Figure 3.3. Administrative structure of the municipality of Sfax

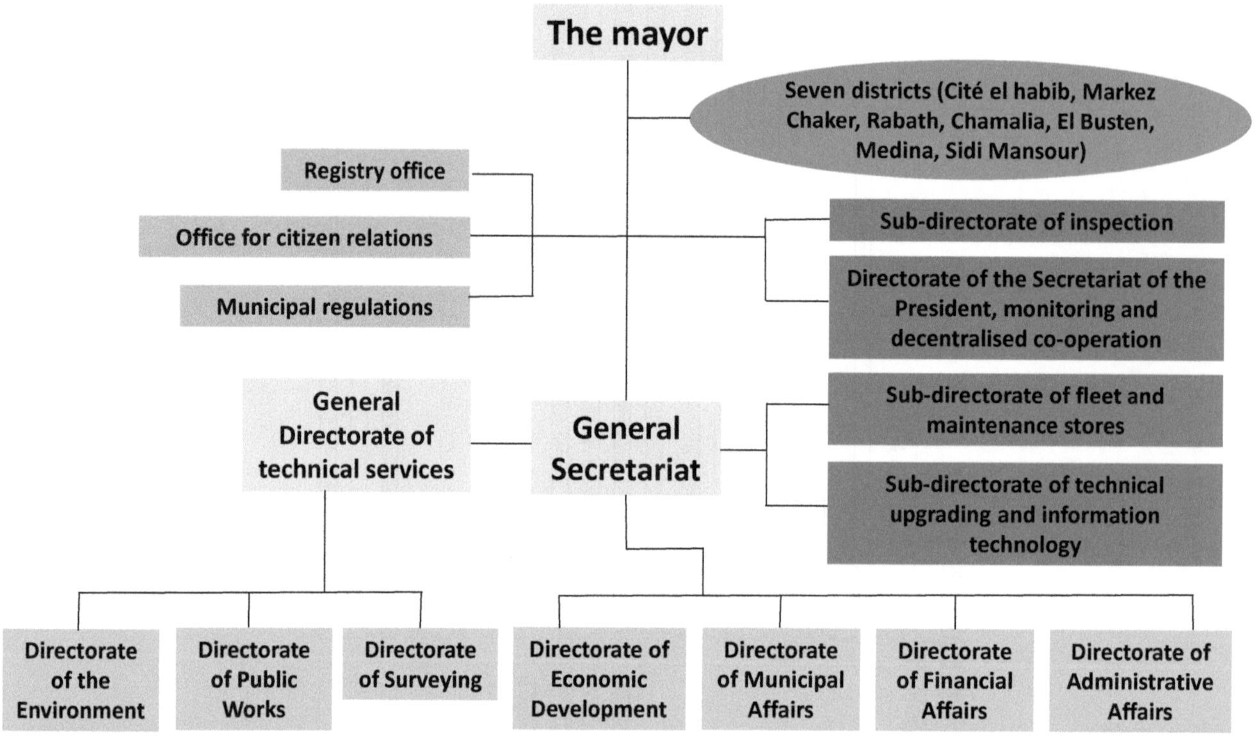

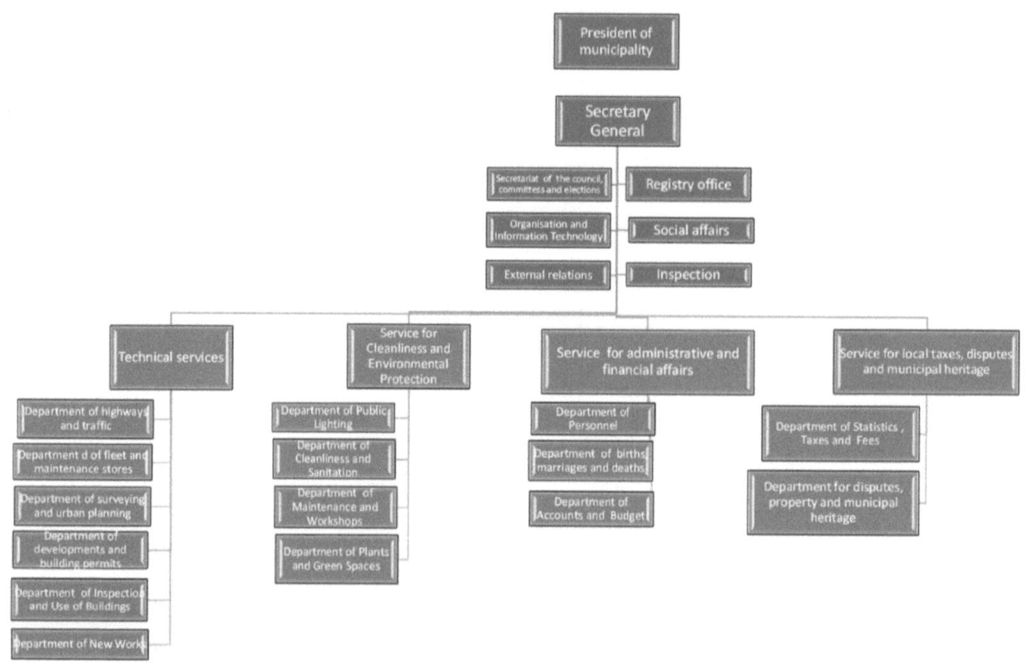

Source: Sfax, 2017, www.commune-sfax.gov.tn/.

Figure 3.4. Administrative structure of the municipality of Sayada

Source: document supplied by the municipality of Sayada.

To respect the new open government requirements, it is critical that the institutional, human and financial frameworks be adapted in the medium and long term. This requires a framework in which the different sections and officials (for access to information, complaints, and the citizens' relations bureau) work in close cooperation and exchange information. The Ministry of Local Affairs and Environment, in partnership with the representative bodies of the municipalities (National Federation of Tunisian Cities and the future High Council of Local Authorities), could draw up proposals on the institutional organisation, based on the experience of open government coordination at the central level in the OECD countries, or on existing structures for citizen participation in cities located in OECD countries (see Box 3.2). These structures should nevertheless be adapted to suit municipalities' size and context.

Box 3.2. "Citizen Relations" Department in the city of Dieppe, France

In Dieppe, this department is "one of the key tools for the citizen participatory process taken by the municipality of Dieppe. Staffed by three officials, it is responsible for developing and implementing tools for local democracy by forming participatory working groups, neighbourhood councils and staging themed city workshops. It offers an interface with citizens, while furthering discussion, thereby assisting them in completing finalised and shared projects. It provides logistical support, particularly for reserving and preparing meeting rooms, and making information or material available. At citizens' request, it facilitates and organises discussions with elected councillors or municipal services to supply them with the information needed for a shared analysis, before helping them access the necessary technical and financial expertise for the projects to be developed, which can subsequently be registered as part of the participatory budgeting process. The team provides support for people of Dieppe wishing to launch neighbourhood micro projects that are eligible for citizen participation funding allocated for activities that focus on building social links and improving community life. It is also tasked with organising and monitoring the functioning of the five neighbourhood councils".

Source: City of Dieppe, (n.d.)

Limited human and financial resources

The success of any open government initiative also depends on the human and financial resources available. For this reason, the OECD Recommendation on Open Government calls on governments to implement reforms by "providing public officials…with adequate human, financial, and technical resources, while promoting a supportive organisational culture" (OECD, 2017a). The Recommendation therefore recognises that open government presents a new culture of governance that requires suitable human and financial skills and resources. For example, interaction with citizens requires skills in negotiation or mediation – skills that the administration could acquire through training offered either by itself, by the national administration, or by partners.

In Tunisia, there are about 800,000 public officials, of whom only 10% are employed at the subnational level. In the OECD countries, the salaries of staff working in local administrations account for 35.7% of public spending in that category (OECD, (n.d.). In Tunisia, the human resources situation in municipalities has further deteriorated due to a recruitment freeze that has been in place since 2011. Furthermore, municipalities are barred from recruiting staff without consent from the supervisory authority, namely the Ministry of Local Affairs and Environment. In Sfax, large numbers of public officials have gone into retirement, and the municipality has been unable to hire new staff. The process of decentralisation under way involves new tasks for the municipalities, and without adequate support, they will face difficulties in implementing projects. This lack of human resources also means that new obligations, such as designating a staff member who is specifically tasked with handling access to information or meeting demands for more effective and transparent communication with citizens, become supplementary duties for public officials. In Sayada, for example, this entails that the financial officer is also responsible for complaints and is the focal point for civil society; meanwhile, the information technology manager is also the focal point for access to information. The municipalities must therefore respond to demands to implement open government initiatives without being able to improve their capacities and expertise in this sector through recruitment. The non-governmental organisation *Action Associative* offered capacity building and training during the introduction of participatory budgeting in La Marsa and Sfax. However, these activities were arranged on an *ad hoc* basis, whereas municipalities need long-term support to be able to meet new demands for access to information, openness, participation and accountability, and to undertake their new prerogatives following the elections and the adoption of the Code for Local Authorities. With this objective in mind, decentralisation allows the level of staff ratio to be increased.

Taking into account the current situation and the recruitment freeze, the national government (Ministry of Local Affairs and Environment as well as the Presidency of the Government), in partnership with civil society and organisations representing the municipalities, could propose training in open government and access to information to support municipalities in the fulfilment of their objectives. Such training would need to be part of an overall approach to training in open government. This process will require the involvement of various actors, such as the National School of Administration, the Centre of Training and Decentralisation Support, or the International Academy for Good Governance. Participation in the OECD Global Network of Schools of Government or cooperation with other international organisations could also promote the development of training programmes. The municipalities themselves are called on to draw up open government approaches that require few human and financial resources. Partnerships with civil society, universities or the private sector – such as those set up in Sayada for management of the website – could also be considered.

Similarly, financial resources at the local level only account for a small share of overall finances. The share of public expenditure for subnational administrations is just 4% (UCLG, 2016) in Tunisia, compared with 40% in the OECD countries (OECD, (n.d.). Of this budget, the majority is used for operations, which limits the budget available for investment (see Figure 3.5, Figure 3.6, Figure 3.7). The municipalities depend on state funding for their operations budget, 75% of which in 2010 came from their own resources and 25% from state funding (Turki and Verdeil, 2015). Interviews with officials and elected representatives from the three municipalities revealed the difficulties in allocating a stable budget that would allow activities linked to open government to be developed at the local level, such as the office for complaints, access to information, or the municipality's strategy for communication and transparency. However, the municipality of Sfax can count on a budget of which 41.6% was allocated to investment in 2017. Funding sources for the municipalities include self-financing, investment loans granted by the CPSCL, and allocations from the national budget. As previously indicated, the municipalities are experiencing difficulties in reaching the levels of self-financing required. The municipality of Sayada claims that it only collects about 10% of taxes. An increase in local tax collection rates could be an effective way of increasing the budget and, as a result, of increasing investment possibilities; however, this step will depend on building greater trust between the municipality and its citizens.

Financial stability and predictability are prerequisites for a long-term vision of open government in the municipalities. This requires greater confidence on the part of citizens in their municipalities, but the national government could also support awareness-raising campaigns to encourage citizens to pay their taxes.

Figure 3.5. Finances of La Marsa in 2016

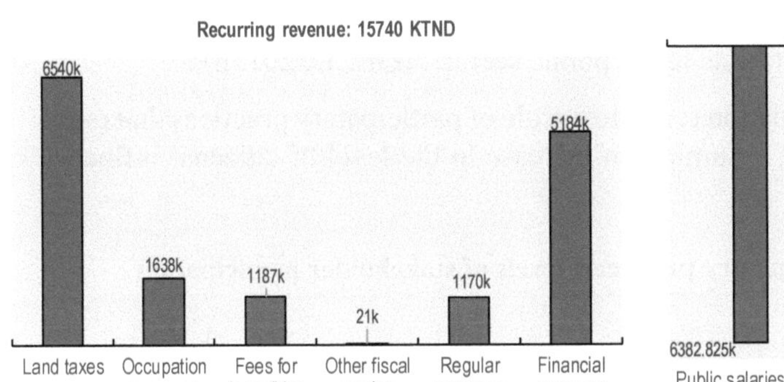

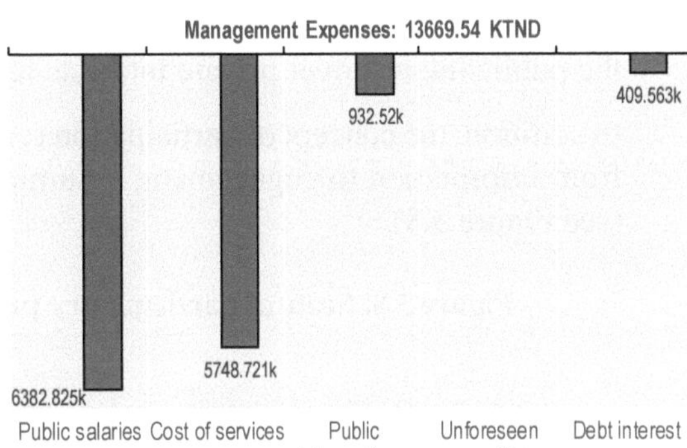

Figure 3.6. Finances of Sfax in 2016

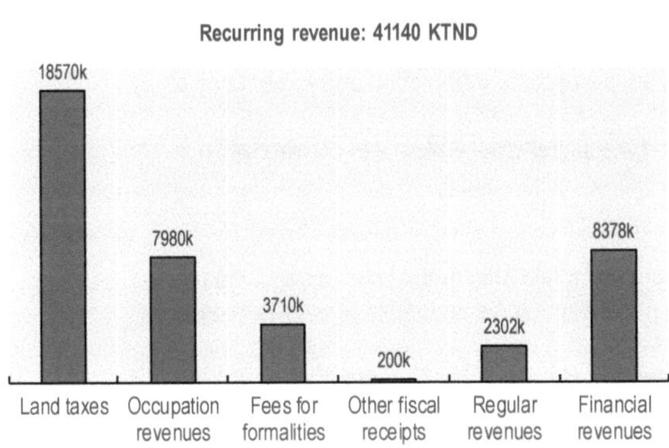

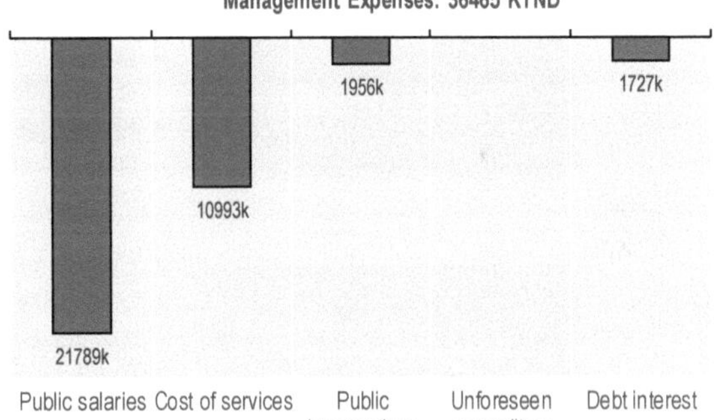

Figure 3.7. Finances of Sayada in 2016

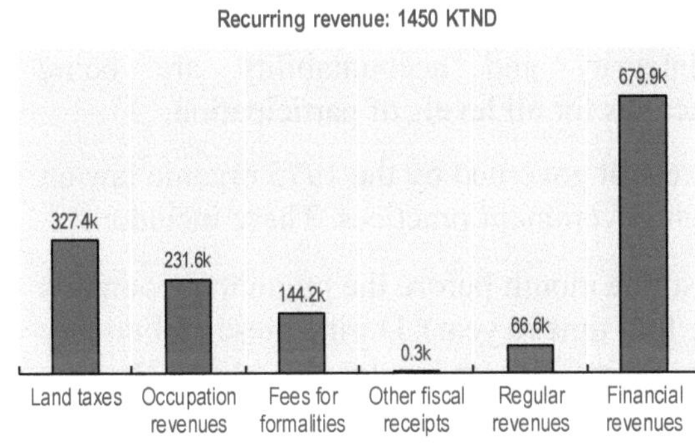

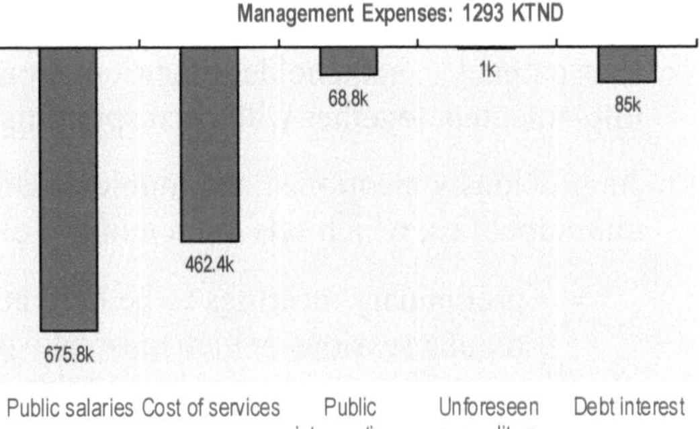

Source: Ministry of Local Affairs and the Environment, 2017.

Open government initiatives and practices in La Marsa, Sayada and Sfax

According to the OECD definition, open government is based on the principles of transparency, stakeholder participation, integrity and accountability. Transparency refers to "the disclosure and subsequent accessibility of relevant government data and information"; participation "typically refers to the involvement of individuals and groups in designing, implementing and evaluating a project or plan"; accountability refers to the government's responsibility and duty to inform its citizens about the decisions it makes as well as to provide an account of the activities and performance of the entire government and its officials" (OECD, 2016a). Public integrity refers to the "consistent alignment of, and adherence to, shared ethical values, principles and norms for upholding and prioritising the public interest over private interests in the public sector". (OECD, 2017b).

In addition, the concept of participation refers to a scale of participatory practices that range from information to engagement, assuming an increase in the level of citizens' influence (see Figure 3.8).

Figure 3.8. Scale of participatory practices: levels of stakeholder participation

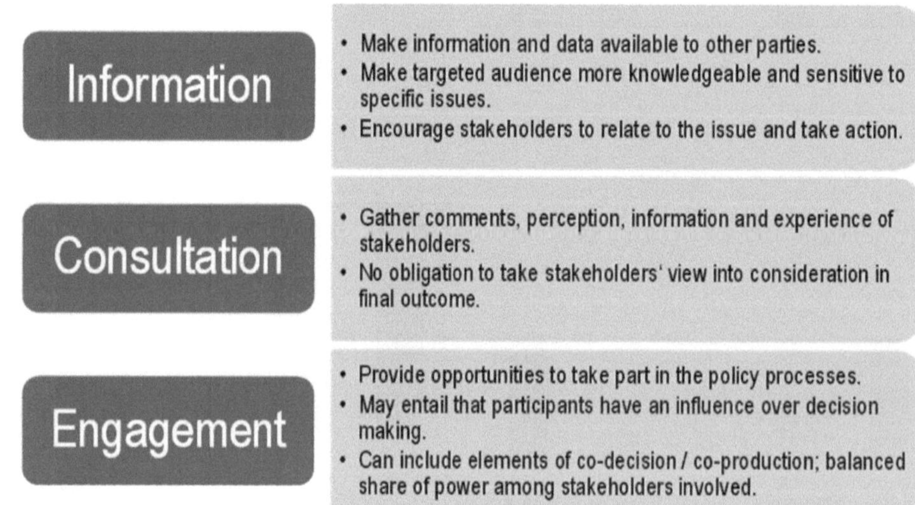

Source: OECD, 2016a.

In the municipalities of La Marsa, Sayada and Sfax, initiatives aimed at establishing transparency, stakeholder participation, integrity and accountability are being implemented, together with corresponding practices for all levels of participation.

As previously mentioned, the municipalities are still governed by the 1975 organic law on municipalities, which sets out a number of open government practices. These include:

- preliminary meetings to be held at least one month before the municipal council's regular sessions (which must take place four times a year). During these preliminary meetings, citizens are invited to express their views on local issues (Art. 32);

- public sessions of the municipal council; the date scheduled must be announced by posting a notice at the entrance to the municipality offices and those of its districts, as well as through various media channels (Art. 39);

- committee meetings to be held at least once a month, which are open to the public; the date scheduled must be announced, by posting a notice at the entrance to the municipality offices, and those of its districts, as well as through various media channels (Art. 14). Public officials and citizens may be called upon to participate in the work of their committees in an advisory capacity (Art.17);

- a transcript of the proceedings of the municipal council session must be posted (Art. 42).

After 2011, the municipalities of La Marsa, Sfax and Sayada implemented these mechanisms and sought to go even further in their efforts to foster constructive dialogue with their citizens. In La Marsa and Sfax, the focus was on participatory budgeting – a tool for joint decision-making together with citizens – which was proposed to the municipalities by *Action Associative*, while in Sayada, priority was given to transparency and surveys.

Transparency

According to Article 15 of the 2014 Constitution, local authorities are required to be transparent. This requirement is underscored by Article 139 of the Constitution, which enshrines the principles of open government – including transparency – as core guidelines for local authorities, as well as by the organic law on the right to access to information, which was adopted in 2016 and entered into force on 24 March 2017. Although the legal framework for transparency has been consolidated since the revolution, the legal framework prior to 2011 included basic requirements in the area of transparency. Law No. 75-33 of 14 May 1975 on municipalities (still in force) stipulates that municipal council meetings, preliminary meetings and committee meetings must be open to the public. However, transparency of government activities was not part of the administrative culture under the regime of Ben Ali. As a result, the municipal administrations and the special delegations appointed in 2011 faced demands for greater openness and transparency. These demands came from citizens and civil society but also the new legal framework– such as the decree law on access to administrative documents, which called for greater transparency.

The long tradition of opacity resulted in the implementation of few transparency mechanisms and processes. The municipality of Sayada was the first to adopt measures for transparency, in response to individual initiatives by citizens. Since 2012, the municipality has published its budget and the proceedings of municipal council meetings online. This new openness was entirely the result of active engagement on the part of citizens, who subsequently grouped together under the banner of the Association for Free Digital Culture (Clibre), which has developed and continues to manage a collaborative online portal for the municipality (villedesayada.tn). Details of the budget, civil status, revenues, proceedings and tenders are published on the website. The partnership also enables civil society to publish information. According to both the municipality and civil society, this new openness has increased trust in the municipality.

The municipalities of La Marsa and Sfax have also taken steps to increase transparency, setting up municipal web portals in mid-2016 in the case of La Marsa (communemarsa.tn) and 2010 in the case of Sfax (commune-sfax.gov.tn), on which certain documents and key data, such as the organisational structure, are published proactively. However, all the municipalities face challenges of inadequate resources to keep their websites updated. In addition, the three municipalities have set up Facebook pages (see Table 3.2), an important communication channel given the importance of Facebook in Tunisia. In the case of

Sayada, the page is jointly managed by civil society. These pages also serve as a platform for publishing information and interacting with citizens.

Table 3.2. Facebook fans on official municipal pages (11 August 2017)

La Marsa	7,021
Sayada	12,066
Sfax	19,598

The municipalities also use more traditional communication methods, such as banners, posters and loudspeakers, as well as briefings with the local media. The proactive approach in the area of transparency is limited to the publication of key documents (proceedings, statistical data, dates of meetings and, in the case of Sayada, monthly expenditures and revenues in open data format). Some open data is also published on the national portal www.collectiviteslocales.gov.tn.

While a culture of open government has been developing since 2011, citizens still find the public administration reluctant to provide access to information. The administration is sometimes guilty of lengthy delays in supplying information, of only publishing certain parts, or refusing to provide data altogether. A case in point was La Marsa, where civil society demanded to see contracts and studies related to the restoration of a bridge in the city. Professional secrecy and liability in cases of unauthorised disclosure may also explain why public officials choose not to release information (Nicolás Adán, J.-E., Ben Hassen, S. and Doggui, 2014). As a result, civil society or citizens are sometimes forced to turn to the judicial system – which in any case involves protracted proceedings and judgements that are not always enforced. Participation in meetings has been cited as one of the most effective means of accessing information about municipal projects under way, such as planning for a central town square.

Since 24 March 2017, municipalities have been obliged to implement the new law on the right to access to information, which replaced the decree law on access to administrative documents. Although the three municipalities have appointed an official with responsibility for access to information, as required by law, the municipalities are finding it difficult to put the new obligations into practice. Following visits in February and March 2017, it emerged that expertise related to the law and the understanding of its implications remain basic, despite some training initiatives conducted in partnership with the OECD. Furthermore, aside from the capacities of the official responsible for access to information (see the section on human resources), the municipalities do not have an appropriate management system for data and archives. Efforts to coordinate the various municipal services should also be improved to foster access to information, particularly in the larger municipalities, such as Sfax. The difficulties do not simply lie in exchanging information between the different services; municipal councillors also report problems in accessing information in Sfax and La Marsa. Furthermore, research carried out by the *Al Bawsala* association, as part of the *Marsad Baladia* project, reveals that the municipalities are not yet in compliance with the new legal framework. The association has drawn up an index for transparency based, among other factors, on the proactive publication of information on the municipality website, and on the rate of response for the information requested by the association (see Table 3.3).

Table 3.3. Transparency rating according to Al Bawsala's Marsad Baladia index

La Marsa	22.6%
Sfax	17.7%
Sayada	46.7%
Radès	86%

Source: Al Bawsala, (n.d.)

Access to information is not just a new obligation for the municipalities. It is also a new right for citizens. However, awareness of this right remains weak among citizens and, as a result, the take-up rate is also low. Although the municipalities do not collect official statistics, they report receiving very few official requests for information. Nevertheless, data from the OECD indicates the importance of measuring the impact of efforts towards transparency. It is crucial that the municipalities improve the process by collecting data on the use of information published, and on the number of requests for information received and handled, while at the same time measuring the impact. Currently, municipalities do not have the financial and human resources to do this.

The municipality index for transparency developed by Transparency International Lithuania reveals the information that Transparency International believes that municipalities should publish proactively. This example could serve as inspiration for Tunisia's municipalities (see Box 3.3).

Box 3.3. Municipality index for transparency

Transparency International Lithuania has developed a municipality index for transparency, which assesses the 60 municipalities of Lithuania based on certain types of information published and made available on their official websites.

The index consists of the following features:

Information on organisational structure

1. list and contact details of employees

2. job descriptions

3. declarations of interest by public officials

4. asset declarations of high-ranking political officials and senior executives

Information on municipal council activities

5. file of individual votes

6. file of individual votes under the previous mandate

7. proceedings of municipal council meetings

8. proceedings of municipal council meetings under previous mandate

Information on anti-corruption policies and activities

9. anti-corruption programme/plan

10. information on tools/initiatives used in anti-corruption programme

---

11. code of conduct

12. policy on travel and accepting gifts

13. information on procedures and methods for whistleblowing

14. information on processes linked to reports submitted by whistle-blowers

15. list of interest groups encountered during service

Information on businesses linked to the municipality

16. list of companies linked to the municipality

17. list of senior executives in businesses

18. proportion of shares held in these companies

19. list of businesses supplying public services in its territory

Information on municipal finances

20. annual budget.

21. annual budget for previous years

22. annual financial reports

23. annual financial reports for previous years

24. municipal debts and reasons for these debts

Information on public procurement

25. planned public procurement

26. technical specifications for corresponding tenders

27. declarations of interest by selection committee

28. list of businesses that win procurement contracts

29. list of services to be procured

30. monetary value of services (to be supplied)

31. justification of selection of successful businesses

32. assets belonging to the municipality and associated rental stream

Information on public participation

33. opportunities and places for public consultation

34. suggestions/comments received during public consultations

35. decisions made following public consultation

36. information on planned council meetings, agendas and related documents

37. information on feedback mechanisms

38. information on processes linked to citizens' suggestions/comments.

Source: Transparency International Lithuania, (n.d.)

Municipalities could consider forming partnerships with local civil society and the media to identify the most important and frequently requested information and data, with a view to their proactive publication. Based on the Sayada model, a partnership can help overcome challenges of limited human and financial resources, and could be useful in ensuring that information is published in a way that is more open and easy to understand.

Such partnerships can also help to spread a culture of transparency, both within the administration and among citizens. The use of seminars, training sessions and information and communication technologies could foster an improved understanding of rights and obligations linked to access to information. To this end, user guides could be developed to outline public officials' obligations, provide case studies and explain the rights and procedures for citizens. Offering prizes to reward transparency, or transparency competitions, could also help to promote a culture of transparency among public officials and spur a spirit of innovation among citizens, civil society and the administration. For this purpose, municipalities would do well to draw on existing experiences in Tunisia at the national level, such as the *Apps for Democracy Hackathons* organised by the *The Tunisian e.Gov Society* association.

Participatory budgeting

"Participatory budgeting is a basic democratic process, through which citizens make decisions in a sovereign and independent manner, in agreement with the municipality, on a share of the budget of their municipality[8]". The first participatory budget was developed in 1989 in the Brazilian city of Porto Alegre as a municipal response to the need to introduce democracy and to address problems posed by traditional labour practices, social exclusion and corruption. As a result, the city experimented with participatory mechanisms to help overcome financial constraints, allow citizens to play a direct role in government activities, and reverse priorities for social spending. It was against this backdrop that participatory budgeting was developed and initially implemented in several Brazilian cities (Shah, 2007). In 2005, participatory budgeting was practised in more than 300 municipalities worldwide. In Tunisia, participatory budgeting was first introduced in 2014 in the four municipalities of La Marsa, Menzel Bourguiba, Tozeur and Gabès, at the initiative of *Action Associative*. In 2015, Manouba, Gafsa and Sfax joined the list, followed, in 2016, by Ben Arous, Kef, Sbeitla and Ettadhamen. Today, 19 municipalities have adopted the participatory budgeting mechanism (Béja, Kélibia, Sidi Bou Said, Nabeul, Monastir, Ariana, Sidi Bouzid and Raoued) (La Presse.tn, 2017). According to *Action Associative*, participatory budgeting "aims to build a relationship of trust between citizens and municipal institutions [...] through citizen participation in the decision-making process [...] and through implementation of mechanisms for transparency and accountability within the municipalities" (*Action Associative*, (n.d.).

Action Associative has supported municipalities in implementing participatory budgeting, using a precise methodology (see Box 3.4). To this end, it has trained both municipal officials and citizens to enable them to serve as facilitators.

Box 3.4. Stages of participatory budgeting in Tunisia

In Tunisia, several municipalities have adopted the participatory budgeting mechanism. Throughout the world, there are a great many different approaches to participatory budgeting. In Tunisia, *Action Associative* is a key actor, that increases awareness and offers training in a well-defined methodology. In line with this system, participatory budgeting takes place according to the following stages.

The process often begins with an official decision by the municipal council to create a budget line for participatory budgeting. Next, an agreement is signed between civil society and the municipality, defining the rules of cooperation.

The first phase is that of communication and raising awareness of the participatory budgeting process and the possibility of engaging in it. Forums are then organised in the various residential areas, hosted on a voluntary basis by local facilitators proposed by signatory associations to the conventions. The facilitators also have the task of informing citizens and raising awareness among them through flyers, messages, broadcasts on loudspeakers, house-to-house visits, etc.

Each forum lasts two days, generally from Saturday to Sunday. The Saturday is devoted to a presentation by the municipality or the technical service about projects planned, achievements and local finances. The Sunday is used for discussions between citizens, allowing them to present their needs and vote for projects. At the end of the forum, three delegates, who must include one woman, one man and one youth, are chosen to represent the residential area/district to which they will be accountable.

After the vote has taken place in all neighbourhoods, a delegates' forum is organised, during which a vote is held for the projects that will subsequently be adopted by the municipal council.

The methodology also provides for the involvement of citizens in the implementation phase. Citizens' monitoring committees are formed to oversee the procurement process and the carrying out of the works.

In addition, several municipalities, including La Marsa, Menzel Bourguiba, Gabès, Tozeur, La Manouba, Sfax and Gafsa, have signed an inter-municipal mutual aid agreement on participatory budgeting. The aim of this inter-municipal network is to provide support and secure its long-term future.

Sources: Jaouahdou, 2016, Action Associative, (n.d.)

In La Marsa, where participatory budgeting was launched under a municipal decree on 9 January 2014, and where in the first round a budget of 550,000 dinars was allocated to public lighting projects, the total participatory budget has now reached 10% of the overall investment budget. In Sfax, on 25 February 2015, the municipal council decided to allocate 3 million dinars of the investment budget to participatory budgeting. In La Marsa, the service categories submitted for participatory budgeting are public lighting, roads, rainwater drainage and pavements, and in Sfax the categories are roads, public lighting and paving. According to the authorities, the participatory process has helped to improve relations between citizens and their local administration and to build a relationship of trust. Participatory budgeting is seen as a means for learning democracy and combating corruption, since it introduces checks and balances, and monitoring by citizens. It has also led to the improvement of infrastructure, by responding to communities' priority needs. However, to build long-term confidence, there is a need for continuity and credibility, especially through the implementation of projects chosen by citizens.

Several years' experience of participatory budgeting in La Marsa, together with the 2015 implementation of this project in Sfax, have highlighted a number of challenges. Despite efforts in the area of awareness raising, and the requirement for at least one delegate to be a youth, officials in La Marsa have pointed to the lack of young people in the process. Furthermore, delays in the implementation and execution of projects is jeopardising the trust that has been created. As for the technical services, officials responsible for implementation are not linked to the participatory budgeting process, which reduces their support for and commitment to dialogue with the citizens. Some have suggested that this self-perpetuating work culture, coupled with the failure to put citizens' and civil society's know-how to good use, is contributing to mistrust between the administration and citizens.

In order to build greater trust with citizens and civil society, it would be useful to increase transparency surrounding municipal operations, especially regarding delays in project implementation. This process requires a systematic approach of monitoring and evaluation of project implementation. For example, the city of Paris, which has adopted the participatory budgeting process, allows citizens to use its website to monitor the implementation of projects that have been voted for. The website indicates whether or not a project has been implemented, and which stage it is currently undergoing (inception, study and design, launch of procedures, project realisation, delivery and inauguration).

Nevertheless, participatory budgeting is a valuable initiative, and one that is judged in positive terms by most administration members and by civil society in La Marsa and Sfax. However, participatory budgeting also carries the risk that open government initiatives will only focus on this process, to the detriment of other municipal operations and more structured activities, such as municipal council meetings and transparency of local government as a whole. In any case, the future of participatory budgeting has been uncertain since the implementation of the process surrounding the annual investment plan within the framework of the PDUGL.

Participatory budgeting enables citizens to decide on specific local projects. Conversely, the AIP required as part of the PDUGL encompasses the entire range of municipal investments, namely local, structural and administrative projects. The AIP methodology stipulates participation, albeit a level of participation – consultation – that gives fewer decision-making powers to citizens than does participatory budgeting, which involves joint decision-making. Since 2016, all municipalities, including those that have adopted participatory budgeting, have a duty to develop their AIP according to the methodology dictated by the CPSCL. However, the experience of participatory budgeting has meanwhile created a community of public officials, municipal councillors and civil society organisations who are convinced of the added value of this practice, and of citizens' right to participate in municipal decision-making, and are persuaded that abrogation of the participatory budgeting process is not an option. The municipalities have therefore attempted to combine the two methods. In La Marsa and Sfax, decisions on local projects have been jointly made with citizens. Indeed, La Marsa had already completed the participatory budgeting process to choose projects prior to the obligatory consultation for the AIP. Citizens' choices therefore formed the basis of the AIP. At present, the co-existence of the two methods is creating confusion. On the one hand, the participatory budgeting process allows stronger participation (joint decision-making, participation in problem diagnosis, assessing project implementation, unlike a public consultation for the

AIP), but on the other, the AIP covers structural and administrative projects to which the participatory budgeting process is unsuited. *Action Associative*, in collaboration with those municipalities that have adopted participatory budgeting, is calling for a merger of the two mechanisms, a prospect that is being opposed by the CPSCL. Given this latter's financial power, it has the means to force municipalities to only apply the AIP.

These developments raise questions about the scope of citizen participation, which should be decided by consensus. Questions include: what should the role of citizens be; to what extent should they participate in management of the municipality? Is citizen participation desirable in the development of structural and administrative projects? Are citizens sufficiently well informed and capable of acting in the public interest? What roles and responsibilities remain with the elected representatives and the municipal council if citizens decide on all investments? Does increased participation in the form of joint decision-making risk forcing a municipality to implement citizens' priorities (or of those citizens who participated) instead of its own priorities, and what are the implications in terms of accountability? At the same time, those municipalities that have experimented with participatory mechanisms cannot turn back, since both civil society and the citizens are demanding their right to participation. As observed by the EU study, "a power struggle has begun to emerge between state actors and civil society over their future roles and prerogatives" (Nicolás Adán, J.-E., Ben Hassen, S. and Doggui, 2014). The Charter of Paris for Citizens' Participation proposes a common framework between the city and its citizens, which sets out the rights and obligations of each (see Box 3.5).

Box 3.5. Charter of Paris for Citizens' Participation

The city of Paris drew up a charter of citizens' participation in 2009, so as to create a common framework and strengthen participation. In the light of developments in terms of citizens' participation since 2009, this Charter has been revised using a participatory process, and a new Charter was adopted in 2018.

The Charter contains the following key points.

TOWARDS PARTICIPATION FOR ALL

1. What participation means.

2. Free and inclusive participation.

3. Participation that is available to everyone.

4. Participation that is more user-friendly.

TRANSPARENCY AND AWARENESS OF PARTICIPATION

5. Transparency and participatory contract.

6. Renewing and connecting citizens' bodies.

7. Strengthening Parisians' role in municipal politics.

FUTURE OF PARTICIPATION AND LIFE OF THE CHARTER

8. Promoting Agoras and public experimentation.

9. Ensuring participatory culture in the long term.

10. Bringing the Charter to life.

Source: Paris City Hall, 2018.

Citizen participation in strategic planning

Participatory budgeting and the AIP are just two participatory mechanisms, albeit currently the foremost topics of debate and those attracting the greatest interest among municipalities and citizens in La Marsa and Sfax. However, citizens' involvement in other municipal processes and decisions is also important.

Participatory budgeting and the AIP only allow participation in a limited share of municipal activities. For example, in Paris, plans are in hand to ensure public consultation on all major municipal projects. Indeed, citizen participation dates back to the 1960s, particularly in the case of urban planning in which citizens demanded the right to be involved. In the wake of the new Constitution, the project for the Code of Spatial Planning and Urban Development (CATU) also provides for a participatory approach to urban planning policy (Articles 40 and 77). Citizen participation was not provided for in either the organic law on municipalities, nor the CATU of 1994. The design of an urban development plan (UDP), which is obligatory for municipalities, therefore represents an opportunity for participation (Turki, S.Y. and Mahjoub, 2014). The plan for the Code for Local Authorities also sets out requirements for a participatory approach to the UDP (Article 228).

1. **Article 40 of the CATU: on the participatory approach.** The development and implementation of urban planning should be conducted using a participatory

approach and in partnership with the various stakeholders involved, particularly through consultation with the councils or committees, where relevant local communities and authorities are represented, as well as with the most representative socio-economic bodies and associations in the area of spatial planning and urban development.

2. **Article 77 of the CATU: on the participatory approach**. A debate may be held within the municipal council on the overall direction of the urban development plan before it is examined by the relevant businesses and public bodies. The debate may bring together residents, local associations and other people concerned throughout the development of the said plan. The president of the municipal council may seek the opinion of anybody or association with competence in the area of land use, urban, environmental, architectural, habitat and transport planning[9].

To date, La Marsa, Sfax and Sayada have not yet developed participatory approaches to drawing up their UDP. La Marsa is currently revising its UDP, a process in which experts and national institutions have been involved. Citizens will have the opportunity to present their views once the plan has been drafted.

Since 2014, the municipality of Sayada has been conducting surveys on its website, allowing citizens to give their opinion, principally on road and infrastructure projects. The results are then presented to the municipal council for adoption. The consultation takes place in several phases: First, a collection of projects is proposed, which the citizens classify according to their preferences; they are then invited to choose the project details. For example, the resurfacing of a number of streets was decided using this mechanism. However, this process is still tainted by a low level of participation and inadequate explanation in the public surveys of the choices and issues at stake. In Sfax, the seven municipalities of Greater Sfax have engaged in a participatory experience in the drafting of the Greater Sfax Development Strategy 2007-2016, which is based on a participatory diagnosis of the present situation (Bennasr, A., Megdiche, T. and Verdeil, 2013; Hadj, 2008).

La Marsa, Sfax and Sayada reflect an innovative spirit in how they have introduced open government practices. It would be useful to draw lessons learned and best practices from this, so that these experiences, as well as the trust built up through participatory budgeting and the partnership in Sayada, can serve as a foundation for enacting structured mechanisms for public consultation and dialogue with all stakeholders affected by major municipal projects and urban development plans. The importance of more structured participation is further underscored by adoption of the Code for Local Authorities and the transfer of new competences to the municipalities. The experiences of participation in strategic planning in the city of Alcobendas in Spain may serve as an inspiration (see Box 3.6).

Box 3.6. Participation in strategic planning in Alcobendas, Spain

In 2013, the municipal council of Alcobendas approved its strategic plan "Diseña Alcobendas 2020". The plan comprises 38 projects divided into five strategic categories (promotion of the city; economic development; innovation; education and employment; sustainable development; good governance, transparent and responsible management; social responsibility and quality of life) which together define a vision for the city.

One of the key objectives was the involvement of all stakeholders in the process. Building on the participatory mechanisms defined in regulations on citizen participation, the plan was developed by following a series of steps:

- Development of an assessment report and a survey of the preferred strategies. These two documents were published on the website and in the local press, and were also explained during roundtable sessions with citizens.

- For each theme, experts were invited to offer advice and help to define public opinion.

- On the basis of this information, working groups using the SWOT methodology were called on to define their vision of Alcobendas, and to propose and develop projects to be included in the strategic plan.

- 513 project proposals were presented in person and through the website, on the initiative of individuals or businesses. These people and companies were then given the opportunity to defend their projects before the public.

- The projects were grouped into themed categories, and stakeholders then classified them by order of priority during the municipal social council, based on two criteria: usefulness for citizens and project viability.

- The final plan was presented to the municipal social committee and approved by the municipal council.

All participants were given feedback on their proposals. A total of 320 people took part in the process, either as individuals or as representatives of institutions, associations or businesses. The entire documentation for the strategic plan is available on this website (www.alcobendas.org/es/portal.do?TR=C&IDR=2295), as are the meeting reports, SWOT analysis, etc. Monitoring and evaluation reports have also been published on the website (city observatory website) to keep citizens informed of the project's state of progress (completed, ongoing, delayed, not activated).

Source: Lino Ramos Ferreiro, Head of Planning and Assessment, Municipality of Alcobendas

Participation in municipal council meetings

The opening of municipal council sessions to the public is current practice in the cities of OECD countries. This public access enables citizens to follow municipal operations closely, to be kept informed and to assess the municipality's capacity to manage the city's affairs. In Tunisia, the municipal council's regular sessions are, in principle, public. Preliminary meetings are organised to enable citizens to express their views. Committee meetings are also public. These clauses are underscored by the Code for Local Authorities, which stipulates that "during municipal council sessions, a place must be left for the media, as well as components of civil society" (Article 219). The municipalities are obliged to inform citizens through various channels.

Despite the importance of council meetings for the running of the municipality, and for the opportunities that they present for participation, the three municipalities – La Marsa, Sfax and Sayada – are seeing a generally low level of participation at meetings, as well as a reluctance to becoming involved and a lack of interest in municipal affairs. Participants are always the same people, who take advantage of the opportunity to voice their grievances. The council meetings are announced via banners and the local press; As for invitations to committee meetings, these are directly extended to the actors concerned – chambers of commerce, trade unions, associations – and, as a result, in municipalities such as Sfax, they attract greater levels of participation. By contrast, Sfax acknowledges that publicity of committee meetings remains inadequate; the calendar is not published in advance and the meetings are organised on a spontaneous basis, thereby reducing the chances of stronger participation. The commitments made by the three municipalities to create better dialogue with citizens and build a climate of trust have nevertheless had a positive impact on participation in council meetings. La Marsa has seen a higher level of participation since participatory budgeting was introduced, especially on the part of citizens involved in it, and in Sayada, citizens are asking the municipal council to hold discussions on certain subjects, such as those concerning the coastal zone. Proceedings of meetings are generally posted in municipal premises, and in some cases are also published on the website. Box 3.7 presents innovative approaches to increasing participation. Municipalities could strengthen their efforts to use information and communication technologies, especially social media networks, to increase participation in municipal council meetings. The municipal councils and their committees will gain in legitimacy following the municipal elections and, as a result will become important places for municipal decision-making. The councillors also organise information centres or open door sessions – common practice in many cities in OECD countries -, which have so far only entailed a low take-up rate.

Box 3.7. Innovative participatory practices using information and communication technologies

Participation in municipal council meetings

In Grenoble, municipal council meetings are aired live on *YouTube*, with sign language. They are available in the website's multimedia library.

Participation via Facebook in Morocco

Through its *Nouabook* project – an online platform that enables visitors to communicate with members of Parliament – the SIM SIM association offers discussions with parliamentarians on Facebook. The debates, which last about an hour, focus on specific themes, such as the issue of women (4th debate), and are available live on Facebook. Citizens can follow the discussions, and leave comments and questions. The debates are succeeding in involving large numbers of the public. The fourth debate (13 July 2017) has been watched more than 60,000 times, and the 3rd one (29 June 2017) has been watched nearly 40,000 times.

Source: City of Grenoble, (n.d.), www.facebook.com/Nouabook/videos/726927920825378/?hc_ref=ARRcj0IjJMDg7DRgZanve5NHBrvcJrI-nXnfOJ9ET8xjEYuGvaKmwZ05I6N6QzyUuuo.

Claims

Claims represent another means of interaction between local government and its citizens. It enables citizens to make their voice heard, as well as their opinion on the quality of the administrative service. The claims system existed long before the revolution. Decree No. 93-982 of 3 May 1993 on the relationship between the administration and its users refers to the obligation to respond to claims regarding administrative services supplied by local authorities. The PDUGL programme calls for an official to be responsible for the complaints management mechanism, whose role is clearly defined in the Guide to Complaints Management Mechanisms. The municipalities receive complaints through various channels, including by post and email, via the citizens affairs office when this exists, and via Facebook. The municipality of La Marsa has also launched a system of lodging online complaints[10], and Sfax receives complaints through local radio stations. In addition, Sfax has set up a website (https://sfax.crowdmap.com/) where citizens can submit claims by specifying the location of the request for intervention on a map of the municipality. The intentions are admirable, but due to the low level of take-up of the mechanisms put in place, results have yet to materialise. None of the three municipalities has the capacity to collect statistics on claims and their responses. Based on their experience, a large proportion of complaints concern the municipal police, and are linked, for example, to infringements related to construction sites. Since 2011, the municipal police has no longer come under the authority of the municipality, with the result that these complaints no longer fall within the municipality's jurisdiction. The police's intervention thus depends on their own discretion. The slow pace of intervention places local government in a delicate situation, as citizens expect rapid responses to their claims.

Participation of specific actors

The participation of specific actors from all social backgrounds and of all ages is a prerequisite to ensure that public policies respond to the needs of everyone, and that each social group has the opportunity to express its opinion and make its voice heard. However, efforts to promote citizen participation at both the national and local level, in Tunisia or in other countries, have encountered challenges. The OECD has identified two main groups that do not participate: stakeholders wishing to but unable to participate, and stakeholders able but unwilling to participate. Additional efforts are therefore required to lower barriers to participation and make the prospect more attractive (OECD, 2009). Box 3.8 identifies various mechanisms used by the Office of Public Consultation of Montreal to broaden participation.

Box 3.8. How to broaden participation in the process of public consultation

The capacity to participate in collective decision-making, and interest in doing so, varies according to individuals. From the perspective of democratic institutions, it is possible to adopt a passive approach – receiving and listening– or an active one, by setting in place various means to obtain the participation of all those concerned by the issues in question.

An active approach is determined from the beginning, during design of the consultation process. It begins by mapping the persons and groups affected by the issue that is the object of the consultation, and by assessing the different obstacles to participation. These may take a number of different forms, such as:

- mistrust of decision-makers;

- lack of information;

- lack of availability

- distance and accessibility of consultation venues;

- lack of interest;

- complexity of forms of participation;

- a feeling of exclusion.

Clearly, there is no form of participation suited to all. It is therefore important to adopt a multi-channel approach.

To illustrate these different methods, listed below are examples of participatory activities that have been organised as part of the consultation framework by the Office of Public Consultation of Montreal (OCPM) on reducing dependency on fossil fuels (http://ocpm.qc.ca/energies-fossiles/).

Public hearings

A format traditionally used by the OCPM, in which citizens or groups sign up to present their opinions before a committee on the theme being debated. This type of participation is formal and allows for relatively expert participation. However, it quite inflexible (fixed venue and time), and some people could find it intimidating to make a verbal presentation in public.

Contributory citizen activities

Takes the form of a facilitation kit that offers an approach and information for addressing the theme being debated. This formula can be easily adapted to suit different groups and may include a playful dimension. It presents no constraints in terms of venue or timetable. The approach has been successfully tested by various groups such as associations, circles of friends, schools, parents' groups, regardless of literacy levels, and at various levels of language proficiency.

Online consultation platform

An online tool that enables users to obtain information about the theme of the consultation and contribute by expressing ideas and opinions. It is easier to reach a large number of participants, particularly if social media networks are used. Citizens have the possibility of participating at any time, and from many place.

Creative Marathon

Creative approaches can be the best way to encourage the participation of some sectors of the public. In the Creative Marathon organised by the OCPM, the objective was to attract contributions to innovation from the community in Montreal. With few contacts in this area and a poor knowledge of some community group practices, representatives were invited to develop the way in which they themselves would like to be consulted. The result was obtained through a series of events similar to Hackathons, during which teams worked to develop prototypes of solutions aimed at reducing dependency on fossil fuels. The final stage involved making a presentation to the committee and city representatives.

Source: Guy Grenier, 2017, Coordinator participatory processes, Office of public consultation of Montreal.

Youth participation

The 2014 Constitution highlights the importance of young people, acknowledging that "youth is an active force in building the nation" and stipulating that the government should "support(s) them to assume responsibility, and strive(s) to extend and generalise their participation in social, economic, cultural and political development." (Article 8). In addition, it stipulates that "the electoral law shall guarantee the representation of youth in local authority councils" (Article 133). Tunisia also recognises that public policies must be designed and implemented with the participation of young people, in order to respond to their needs and make them agents of national and local development. However, in terms of citizen participation, the praiseworthy initiatives of La Marsa, Sfax and Sayada have not succeeded in involving youth. According to interviews conducted during missions in February and March, municipal representatives have observed that in a general sense, there is a lack of active mobilisation and participation of youth on the themes discussed during debates on participatory budgeting and during council meetings, despite the requirement that one of the three participatory budgeting delegates should be a young person. The youth centres belong to the municipalities, and could be a place for interaction with young people, but these places come under the authority of the Ministry for Youth and Sports, requiring direct coordination between the municipality and the national administration. In Sayada, the youth centre has been under construction for two years, restricting venues for youth activities. The CoMun project implemented by GIZ is attempting to respond to the challenges of a local policy of integration and inclusion by offering training in the involvement of young people and developing joint projects between the municipalities and youth. As part of the national action plan for open government, the Ministry for Youth and Sports has pledged to set up youth councils at the local level. All these initiatives can help to develop more consistent approaches and strategies for engaging young people in municipal life. "Think young" involves shaping communication to target youth, using channels that speak to them, implementing innovative participatory structures, presenting municipal issues in a way that makes them relevant and building youth's capacity in the field. Box 3.9 presents several best practices to promote youth participation in the municipalities of OECD countries. Targeted actions are needed to include young people and marginalised groups. Partnerships with associations that represent these could help to involve them more closely.

Box 3.9. Innovative practices for involving youth in municipalities

In Paris, France, the **Parisian Youth Council,** launched in 2003, is a body for participatory democracy. It aims to connect young Parisians with the development of municipal policies, to inform municipal decision-making so that it takes greater account of the needs and expectations of young Parisians, and to help the city in designing innovative solutions to support young Parisians in becoming autonomous. It is made up of 100 young people aged 15 to 30, who meet in plenary session twice a year and at meetings for different works. The candidates are chosen by drawing lots. The Mayor of Paris may summon the Council to obtain its opinion on various subjects that are presented to the municipal councillors.

In Belgium, "Youth Centres" are associations set up at the local level with the aim of promoting the development of a citizenship that is critical, active, responsible and supportive, principally among young people between the ages of 12 and 26, through increased awareness and knowledge of the realities of society, as well as attitudes towards

---

responsibility and participation in social, economic and cultural life. These centres develop a local youth policy and encourage the implementation and promotion of socio-cultural and creative practices. The activities in which the associations choose to invest are highly diverse. There is a particular focus on actions or projects related to artistic practices, to the issue of equal opportunities, information and communication technologies and alternative sports practices, etc. Some youth centres are involved in spurring initiatives linked to local development, such as organising municipal youth councils, homework support, or outreach activities for young people in vulnerable situations.

In Quebec, youth centres that are members of the *Regroupement des maisons de jeunes du Québec (RMJQ),* (Youth Centres Group of Quebec) are associations of young people and adults who have undertaken, on a voluntary basis, to provide a vibrant a meeting place in their communities where young people aged 12 to 17 can develop their capacities and knowledge in the area of citizenship. It offers youth the possibility of taking responsibility and engaging in projects based on cultural, educational and sporting activities and health awareness-raising, information and promotional initiatives, which they find interesting and are designed to be useful to the community.

Sources: Paris City Hall, (n.d.) and other sources in Belgium and Quebec.

Towards a relationship of trust between citizens and local government

These participatory initiatives are laudable given that, before the revolution, direct communication between citizens and local government was not part of the political and administrative culture. However, such initiatives are affected by a lack of mutual trust: first and foremost, since the time of the former regime, citizens have harboured a mistrust of the political and administrative class. The fact that the government is delaying implementation of local democracy and continues to face problems of corruption diminishes its credibility among the Tunisian people. In addition, the administration lacks confidence in citizens who fail to pay all their local taxes, and towards civil society, accused by some of serving particular interests. A study conducted by the European Union in 2014 identified similar challenges. These challenges to participatory democracy include:

- "The feeling of low willingness to cooperate on the part of state actors;

- The feeling of poor consideration of civil society by state actors, who accord it little attention;

- The feeling of instrumentalisation of associations by state actors;

- The feeling of scant willingness to cooperate with civil society organisations on the part of state actors;

- The feeling that civil society is attempting to serve its own interests more than general interests;

- The feeling of lack of legitimacy and representativeness on the part of civil society" (Nicolás Adán, J.-E., Ben Hassen, S. and Doggui, 2014).

Municipalities and civil society are attempting to break with the culture of closed government and to set up new mechanisms for interaction. This commitment has helped to drive practices for open government, but additional efforts will be required to establish a new culture and to make open government the guiding principle of local administration. A common vision of the roles of each actor, of local government, citizens and civil society will help to embed a culture of open government. The Code for Local Authorities can also contribute in this respect, since it sets out a large number of mechanisms for transparency, participation and accountability, and acknowledges the importance of citizens, civil society and the media in municipal affairs. In particular, it highlights participatory democracy as the way in which municipal affairs should be managed. The inclusion of open government principles in the legal framework also exists in other countries of the MENA region and the OECD, and they can help to strengthen implementation of these practices. Examples include Organic Law No. 113-14 on municipalities, adopted by Morocco in 2015, which contains provisions for promoting transparency, participation and accountability. Chapter V on participatory mechanisms for dialogue and consultation should also be mentioned. It calls for participatory mechanisms for dialogue and consultation, as well as the setting up of a consultative body. The New Zealand law on local authorities (2002) contains provisions on participation, including for consultation (Article 82), and Article 5 of the Municipal Code of Costa Rica provides for the active participation of the population. Box 3.10 lists the most important prerogatives for open government in the Code for Local Authorities in Tunisia.

Box 3.10. Most important open government prerogatives in the Code for Local Authorities

The Code devotes an entire chapter (Chapter 5) to participatory democracy and open governance. In addition, the text contains clauses throughout on transparency, citizen participation and accountability.

Chapter 5: Participatory democracy and open governance

- In the establishment of territorial use and development programs, local authorities must make use of the mechanisms of participatory democracy.

- The local authority council ensures effective participation for all residents and civil society during the various phases of preparation of the territorial use and development programs, and their monitoring, implementation and evaluation.

- The local authorities can refuse any development programmes that go against the provisions of this article. Any decision taken by the local authority in violation of the provisions of this article may be appealed by way of prosecution for excess of power.

- The local authorities maintain a registry of civil society members concerned by local affairs.

- The local authority has a special register for "citizens' opinions" and responses to their questions.

- Organisational projects are published 15 days before discussion by the elected councils.

- The local authority council can organise a referendum on preparation of programmes and implementation of projects falling within its competence.

- One-tenth of the citizens residing in the local authority can also propose organisation of a referendum. There can be no more than one referendum during the municipal or regional term. The governor may oppose the organization of the

---

referendum before the administrative court of first instance within a period not exceeding one month from the date of his notification.

- The proactive approach is compulsory in the areas of transparency and access to information concerning:

  o   projects for local authority regulatory decisions;

  o   financial management;

  o   property management

  o   contracts entered into by the local authority;

  o   works and investments planned by the local authority.

- The local authorities work, in partnership with the National Institute of Statistics, on drafting a local statistical database.

- The municipal and regional councils can organise public meetings with citizens, during which the council will provide clarification and the citizens will submit their proposals before the adoption of decisions on certain themes.

- A meeting can also be organised following the filing of a reasoned request by at least 10% of citizens registered on the municipal or regional electoral roll.

- The presidents of local councils and their members with responsibility for various tasks must declare their assets and interests.

Among other clauses stipulating open governance are the following points on transparency in municipal management:

- The principle of transparency and participation in preparation of the budget (Article 130);

- An excerpt of the minutes of discussions to be posted and inserted on website (Article 224).

Participatory mechanisms during development of municipal activities:

- The principle of open government in public service management (Article 75);

- The local development plan (Article 105), the investment programme, the municipal equipment programme (Article 238) and urban development plans (Article 239) are to be drawn up using the mechanism of participatory democracy;

- Commissions are to adapt the mechanism of participatory democracy (Article 212).

And the important role of citizens, civil society and the media:

- The municipality can set up a special committee composed of civil society representatives with responsibility for monitoring operations of public services (Article 78);

- Each district sets up a consultative committee (Article 229);

- Two new commissions are to be set up, for participatory democracy and open governance and media, communication and assessment (Article 210);

> - During municipal council sessions, a place is reserved for the media, as well as for civil society organisations (Article 219).
>
> *Source:* Code for Local Authorities

With the aim of fulfilling these new responsibilities and addressing the challenge of mistrust, municipalities could consider engaging in dialogue with civil society to establish a common charter/vision, based, for example, on the charter adopted for participatory budgeting, and a roadmap to apply the clauses on open government included in the Code for Local Authorities. This process would enable enlarging the participatory mechanisms used (see Table 3.4).

Table 3.4. Participatory mechanisms

Name of initiative	Objective	Nature of topics addressed	Organiser	Duration/Number of participants
Public meeting of 21st century	Advise decision-makers using modern technologies	Mainly local issues, such as municipal development	Municipality, agencies	1 day/500-5,000
Evaluation survey	Stimulate a process of change, on the basis of previous successes	Process of change in organisations and society	Businesses, municipalities, agencies	Flexible
Citizens' forum	Strengthen democratic competences, launch a social debate	Discussions on the subject of regional, national and transnational issues	To date, only private foundations	Several weeks/300-10,000
Participatory budgeting	Encourage citizens to participate in budgetary decisions	Defining priorities and spending and consolidating local and municipal budgets	Local elected representatives, local government	Several months/up to 10,000
Citizens' panel	Advise decision-makers	Views given to politicians and service providers, long-term change in public opinion	Local elected representatives and other stakeholders	3-4 years (up to 4 annual panels)/500-2,500
Citizens' council	Influence debates in society, advise decision-makers	Municipal development and local issues	Local elected representatives, local government, clubs, businesses	Monthly two day meetings/small groups of 8-12 people
Deliberative polling	Transfer of information, discussion	Wide range of issues at the local and transnational level	Political decision-makers	Several weeks/300-500
European citizens consultation	Transfer of information, discussion, influencing social debate	Future of Europe, local and European issues	Political agencies and decision-makers	Several months/ different groups of 25-150 people, up to a total of 1,800
Consensus conference	Exchanges between experts and non-experts	Controversial issues of public, interest at local and transnational level	Agencies	3 days (+2 weekends for preparation)/10-30

Forum on national issues	Transfer of information, skills acquisition	Different issues regarding public organisation at the local or national scale	Municipalities, schools, universities and other educational institutions	1-2 days/10-20
Open conference	Reflect and launch new ideas	Virtually any issue that calls for a new or creative idea	Businesses, clubs, agencies, municipal institutions, educational institutions, churches, etc.	1-3 days/flexible (10-2,000)
Planning for a real exercise	Reorganise common spaces	Urban planning projects	Local elected representatives, local government, similar institutions	Several months/ flexible
Planning unit	Integrate citizens' knowledge into planning decisions	Problems of local and regional planning (urban planning, infrastructure)	Local elected representatives, local government, similar institutions	2-4 days/flexible (max. 25 people per planning unit)
Technical scenario	Compare different future scenarios	Anticipation of future developments and formulation of recommendations on different topics, from local to transnational level	Businesses, clubs, institutions, local government, educational institutions, churches, etc.	1-3 days/flexible (25-250, max. 30 people per group)
World café	Mobilise collective intelligence	Virtually any issue that calls for a new or creative idea	Businesses, clubs, institutions, local government, educational institutions, churches, etc.	Flexible (3 hours to 2 days)/flexible (12-1,200)
Conference for the future	Develop common perspectives, accepted by all stakeholders	Long-term strategies and objectives for organisations and society	Businesses, municipalities, institutions	2-3 days/ ideally, group of 64
Future workshop	Adopt a creative approach to resolving complex problems, developing common perspectives about the future	Long-term changes and guiding processes and projects	Municipalities, institutions, organisations, clubs, etc.	2-3 days/flexible (max. 25 people per group)

Although this discussion process may be tailored to each municipality, exchanges between municipalities could serve to inspire each other. A dialogue with national government, which currently prepares a legal framework for public consultations, could also prove useful in defining a common vision. These dialogues at the local and national level will help to develop a common vision of citizen participation in Tunisia. In order to ensure continuity, civil society and public officials will be called on to share their experiences and best practices with the new municipal council.

The voluntary sector, social movements and the media

Active citizen participation in municipal development, as well as citizens' capacity to demand accountability from the municipality, will partly depend on the voluntary sector and the media.

Freedom of association is a constitutional right (Article 35). It is regulated by Decree-Law No. 2011-88 of 24 September 2011 on the organisation of associations, which, following the 2011 Revolution, stipulated conditions for freedom of association. Since then, Tunisia has seen the creation of a large number of civil society organisations; in May 2017, more than 20,000 associations were registered in the Official Gazette of the Republic of Tunisia. However, according to officials from the jamaity.org platform, only about 3,000 associations are truly active, and of these, a large number rely on international funding

(Robert, 2016). In addition, an EU report observes that, despite the existence of associations with a certain level of professionalism and technical expertise, many of them lack these attributes and take the form "albeit in a relative manner, of a position of beneficiary vis-à-vis the Government and its administration", following a culture inherited from the old regime (Nicolás Adán, J.-E., Ben Hassen, S. and Doggui, 2014).

Of all the civil society organisations in Tunisia, about 20% are registered in the governorate of Tunis where La Marsa is located, 8% are in the governorate of Sfax, and 4% are in the governorate of Monastir, where Sayada is located. Most of the associations operate in the areas of education, culture and art, and only 3.19% are active in the area of citizenship (Centre for Information and Training, 2017).

According to officials in La Marsa, this municipality can count on about 400 associations. A coalition of civil society organisations for La Marsa (see Figure 3.9), which groups together 16 associations into a network, has signed a common charter, enabling the collective implementation of initiatives. This type of network not only facilitates the activities of civil society, but also engagement with the municipality.

Figure 3.9. Coalition of civil society organisations in La Marsa

Source: www.facebook.com/CASCMarsa/?ref=py_c.

The number of associations in Sayada is estimated at about 23, half of which were set up after 2011. However, not all the associations and their members are active. In Sayada, a number of associations – between 8 and 10 – are working together to launch and implement long-term projects with the municipality, particularly on the coast or in the fishing port. For these associations, lack of meeting spaces poses a challenge to their activities. Sfax has a civil society that is highly dynamic. In addition, the municipality supports associations by allocating them funds to finance their activities. As described in Box 3.11, support for associations from the State or municipalities is common practice in OECD countries.

Box 3.11. Support for civic action in French municipalities

In many French municipalities, the city offers support to civic action, in order to encourage it. This includes financial assistance, as well as expertise, assistance and making available tools and facilities.

The city of Champigny-sur-Marne supports civic action through:

1. "Support to administrative procedures, assistance to project organisers.

2. Making available tools and methodological support.

3. Subsidies and in-kind assistance (loan of rooms, gymnasiums, materials…).

4. Promoting the actions of associations and volunteers, and support in staging events."

In Clamart, this support includes management advice to associations, as well as assistance in launching them and training for leaders.

The municipality of Aubervilliers, which awards grants to associations, requires that they respect certain criteria, including the following:

5. "The association must be declared to the Prefecture and registered with a SIRET code.

6. Association actions must be for the benefit of citizens of Aubervilliers and linked to community life.

7. The association must not be religious or political.

8. The association must respect management rules that are disinterested and not-for-profit, and operate in a democratic manner, without discrimination, fostering the equal participation of men and women, as well as that of different generations.

9. The association undertakes to supply the City with a balance sheet and a report on its activities endorsed by a general assembly within six months of the end of the fiscal year."

Sources: Municipality of Champigny-sur-Marne, (n.d.), Municipality of Clamart, (n.d.), Community life-Portal of associations of Aubervilliers, (n.d.).

In a context of transition, in which the country waited several years for local elections, it is unsurprising that a number of associations have been accused of being politicised and of wanting to stand for election. Some public actors explain their mistrust of civil society organisations by the fact that they believe that some associations play the *de facto* role of political parties (Nicolás Adán, J.-E., Ben Hassen, S. and Doggui, 2014). As a result, developing a culture of transparency, not just within municipalities, but also in the non-profit sector, becomes increasingly imperative. It would therefore be useful to establish standards for transparency and accountability. Exchanges between Tunisian associations, as well as with international ones, could serve to define a charter of associations, which would include points on financial transparency and conflicts of interest.

In addition to associations, there are also neighbourhood committees. These date back to the 1990s and were first launched in 1991 during a Ministerial Council session. The neighbourhood committees were considered "a dynamic bridging point between decision-makers and citizens" and their objective was "the mobilisation and participation of citizens to improve neighbourhood living conditions, especially by involving its members in municipal life, notably through their participation in municipal councils, where they will represent citizens' interests". The neighbourhood committees have also been very active in the areas of cleanliness and the environment. However, during the time that Ben Ali was in power, these committees were reported to have been co-opted and used by the Democratic Constitutional Rally (RCD) for control and propaganda purposes (Nicolás Adán, J.-E., Ben Hassen, S. and Doggui, 2014). After 2011, the neighbourhood committees continued to exist, and their role is in the process of being redefined.

Citizen engagement is also expressed through other channels, such as social movements or citizens' protests, which increased significantly in Tunisia in 2017, particularly with regard to regional disparities and regional development. These movements are particularly prominent in the south of Tunisia, but supporting movements have also been formed in a number of governorates, including those of Tunis, Sousse and Sfax. In May 2017, the main focus of group protests was on economic, social, political, administrative and security issues, but at other times, educational and health issues have also been important topics, especially in January 2017. The targets of protest movements have included the governorates, delegations and security bodies, sports stadiums, ministers and the Presidency of the Government, the municipalities and ARP (FTDES, 2017). Tunisia also experienced a wave of protest movements in early 2018 following the adoption of the budget law.

These movements demonstrate the existence of a significant degree of citizen mobilisation in Tunisia, and a level of participation in other places and through other means. However, as everywhere in the world, the citizen participation encouraged by the public administration revolves around an invitation to take part in institutionalised participatory processes related to challenges identified by the public authorities. Citizens are seldom encouraged to launch participatory processes in a proactive manner, and to define the challenges themselves (Schauppenlehner-Kloyber and Penker, 2016). With the exception of a few associations, a lack of initiative on the part of citizens and associations has been identified as a challenge in La Marsa, Sayada and Sfax. Nevertheless, a number of cities around the world, such as Berlin and Paris, offer examples of collective action, self-organisation and joint resource management, including participatory gardens and neighbourhood groups. Another channel for interaction with civil society is through local citizen councils, as in the case of Latin America (see Box 3.12).

Box 3.12. Local citizen councils in Latin America

Since the 1980s, the Latin American public authorities have forged a new relationship with their citizens, allowing them to play a more active role in the decision-making process. The fact that they have succeeded is partly due to the launch of local citizen councils.

Although the local councils take different names and formats within Latin America, they share common features. In a general, they group together representatives of different sectors of civil society, such as the university sector, civic or local organisations and the private sector, and they connect these with representatives of local political authorities within a single body, where, working together, they develop public policies or development programmes. They generally pursue a common objective: strengthening democracy and improving the quality and responsiveness of public policies at the local level.

In certain cases, the setting up of local councils is provided for by the Constitution (for example the Constitution of Peru, Article IV, Chapter XIV on decentralisation) or a national law (for example the Mexican national law on water, which provides for the establishment of Basin Councils). In other cases, councils have been set up on the initiative of local government and citizens (for example in Colombia, with the youth municipal councils of Medellin).

In general, the local councils of Latin America are made up of elected representatives from different social, political and sometimes economic sectors, showing the importance of the capacities and goodwill of actors participating in the councils, and in particular, the attitude adopted by local government regarding citizen participation. The local councils of Latin America follow two main models, depending on the range of thematic areas that they handle. The first model allows local councils to examine and draft overall development plans that cover a variety of sectorial challenges, such as the Concerted Development Plan of Peru (*Plan de desarrollo concertado*). Under the second model, local councils are created to address specific thematic areas, such as social policy, environmental protection, urban governance or public service delivery, as in the case of the local health councils in Paraguay.

Source: OECD, 2016b.

This type of action offers an opportunity for citizens to participate in the debate on issues related to municipal development and its design (Schauppenlehner-Kloyber and Penker, 2016). At the same time, institutionalised participatory processes offer a means for social movements to express their demands in a different manner. For example, in Berlin, Germany, social movements used a referendum in 2013 to make their demands heard about the re-municipalisation of electricity, and again in 2014, about the use of the old Tempelhof airport (Lebuhn, 2015). Social movements have the potential to propose participatory means that go beyond the systems established by institutions, and to mobilise non-organised citizens (Martínez, 2010), as has also been seen in Tunisia. Careful thought about how best to integrate social movements in municipal efforts to promote open government can only enrich and broaden citizen participation (Neveu, 2011). Box 3.13 presents other approaches that could help to extend participation.

Box 3.13. Participatory mechanisms –excerpt from the Guide to Best Practices for Local Governance

- "Where necessary, strengthen citizens' capacities and sense of initiative (bottom-up and top-down participation). This objective could, for example, be achieved by setting up counselling sessions with the aim of introducing a service known as proximity-citizenship. Such a service can be illustrated through the example of citizen centres located in the neighbourhoods of French towns and cities. These are meeting places run by people working in local services, as well as neighbourhood councillors and residents' groups.
- Activate the role of planning advisory committees and give them greater authority and prerogatives. These are committees made up of citizens and business representatives, chosen by local elected officials. They can be considered as a source of proposals, as well as a lobbying group.
- Promote the role of arbitration bodies (customary and state-based) to resolve local land disputes and facilitate access to land, especially in rural regions that agree to accept new development projects. These bodies may be assisted by "strategic groups" made up of figures who enjoy social recognition, and have significant political weight and influence in the local environment where land disputes are occurring".

Source: IACE, 2015.

Local media also offers the potential for implementing open government. Media often serves as a bridge between the public administration, government and citizens by providing information on public policies and demanding accountability from the administration. Since 2011, which saw the liberation of the press, Tunisia's media sector has undergone a significant transformation. Indeed, Tunisia has seen the emergence of new media at the national and local levels in print and online news services, as well as in the audio-visual sector. Legal recognition of community radio stations, defined as radios that are "specialised, local, not-for-profit and serve the interest of the general public", and the launch of several radio stations of this nature demonstrates the importance attributed to the local media for public debate and citizen participation. However, of the ten radio stations recognised by the High Independent Authority of the Audio-Visual Commission (HAICA), three are in the region of Grand Tunis (Radio Campus, Media Libre FM, Radio 6), but none are in Sfax or Sayada. In these regions, public local radio stations (Radio Sfax and Radio Monastir), together with private radios (including *Jawhara FM* in Monastir and *Radio Diwan* in Sfax) are important sources of local information. Both the governorate and the municipality of Monastir frequently use Radio Monastir to discuss and convey information on local issues, such as cleanliness, public lighting and transport (GIZ, 2014). As previously mentioned, radio is also used in Sfax to convey citizens' opinions and demands to the municipality. A radio station is currently being set up in La Marsa[11].

At a time when community radio, including web radio stations, is emerging in Tunisia, as well as online press, local authorities would do well to promote dialogue with these media channels to help them become active players in discussions between society and government. By making press contacts and facilitating direct access to information – without having to pass through central government – municipalities can encourage a type of journalism that pays closer attention to local issues.

References

(n.a.) (2015), "Rapport Revue Mission d'évaluation de la performance de la gestion des finances locales à la Municipalité de SFAX selon la méthodologie PEFA", http://www.collectiviteslocales.gov.tn/wp-content/uploads/2016/11/TN-Sfax-PEFA.pdf (accessed on 30 January 2018).

Al Bawsala (n.d.), Marsad Baladia, http://baladia.marsad.tn/fr/classement/transparence (accessed on 29 January 2018).

Bennasr, A., Megdiche, T. & Verdeil, E. (2013), "Sfax, Laboratoire du développement urbain durable en Tunisie?", Environnement Urbain/Urban Environment, Vol. 7, pp. 83-98, http://www.vrm.ca/wp-content/uploads/EUE7_Bennasr.pdf (accessed on 29 January 2018).

Businessnews (2015), Monastir : Démission collective de la délégation spéciale de Sayada | Businessnews.com.tn | Journal électronique de Tunisie, http://www.businessnews.com.tn/monastir--demission-collective-de-la-delegation-speciale-de-sayada,520,59829,3 (accessed on 29 January 2018).

Centre d'Information, de Formation, D. (2017), Tableau Général des Associations au 28 Novembre 2017, http://www.ifeda.org.tn/stats/francais.pdf (accessed on 30 January 2018).

City of Dieppe (n.d.), Direction relation aux Citoyens, http://tablet.dieppe.fr/menus/la-mairie-5/services-municipaux-82/la-direction-de-la-democratie-locale-et-de-la-citoyennete-276 (accessed on 30 January 2018).

City of Grenoble (n.d.), Retransmission des conseils municipaux - Grenoble.fr, http://www.grenoble.fr/417-retransmission-des-conseils_municipaux.htm (accessed on 30 January 2018).

CPSCL (2015), Guide sur la consultation publique pour les collectivités locales, http://www.collectiviteslocales.gov.tn/wp-content/uploads/2015/06/GUIDE-de-la-consultation-publique.pdf (accessed on 29 January 2018).

Die Landesregierung Nordrhein-Westfalen (2014), Die Open.NRW-Strategie, https://open.nrw/sites/default/files/atoms/files/opennrwt1web.pdf.

FTDES (2017), Rapport mai 2017 des mouvements sociaux, Rapport de l'Observatoire Social Tunisien Mai 2017, https://ftdes.net/fr/ost-rapport-mai-2017-mouvements-sociaux/ (accessed on 30 January 2018).

GIZ (2014), La démocratie locale et la participation des citoyens à l'action municipale: Tunisie.

Guidara, A. (2015), Le Budget Participatif: Un pas vers la démocratie locale en Tunisie (l'expérience de la commune de Sfax), Leaders, http://www.leaders.com.tn/article/18292-le-budget-participatif-un-pas-vers-la-democratie-locale-en-tunisie-l-experience-de-la-commune-de-sfax (accessed on 29 January 2018).

Hadj, M. (2008), Stratégie de Développement du Grand Sfax 2016, http://www.medcities.org/documents/21762/49931/8.STRAT%C3%89GIE+DE+D%C3%89V%C3%89LOPPEMENT+DU+STRATEGIE+DEVELOPEMENT+DURABLE+GRAND+SFAX+2016-+MR.+MOHAMED+HADJ+TA%C3%8FEB.pdf/91d6e854-bb2f-4ed1-a3e1-1cc3f96807fa (accessed on 29 January 2018).

IACE (2016), Rapport sur l'Attractivité Régionale 2016, http://www.iace.tn/wp-content/uploads/2017/01/Rapport-attractivite-regionale-2016-.pdf (accessed on 29 January 2018).

IACE (2015), Guide de Bonnes Pratiques de Gouvernance Locale,
http://www.iace.tn/wp-content/uploads/2017/02/Guide_gouvernance-locale_version-finale.pdf
(accessed on 29 January 2018).

Jaouahdou, K. (2016), Le Budget Participatif en Tunisie: Développement numérique et perspectives,
Action Associative, http://www.aegid-foundation.org/events/archives/0/interventions/9
(accessed on 30 January 2018).

La Presse.tn (2017), Action municipale: A l'heure du budget participatif,
http://www.lapresse.tn/index.php?option=com_nationals&task=article&id=131922
(accessed on 29 January 2018).

Lebuhn, H. (2015), Urban Social Movements between Protest and Participation,
http://www.rc21.org/en/wp-content/uploads/2014/12/E10.1-Lebuhn.pdf
(accessed on 29 January 2018).

Mairie de Champigny sur Marne (n.d.), Le soutien à la vie associative,
http://www.champigny94.fr/associations/le-soutien-la-vie-associative (accessed on 30 January 2018).

Mairie de Clamart (n.d.), Soutien aux associations,
http://www.clamart.fr/loisirs/vie-associative/soutien-aux-associations (accessed on 30 January 2018).

Mairie de Paris (2018), La Charte parisienne de la participation est adoptée – Paris.fr,
https://www.paris.fr/actualites/consultation-numerique-charte-parisienne-de-la-participation-4580
(accessed on 30 January 2018).

Mairie de Paris (n.d.), Le Conseil Parisien de la Jeunesse,
https://www.paris.fr/participez/proposer-et-debattre/devenir-un-acteur-de-la-participation-3934#le-conseil-parisien-de-la-jeunesse_5
(accessed on 30 January 2018).

Martínez, M. (2010), "The Citizen Participation of Urban Movements in Spatial Planning: A Comparison between Vigo and Porto", International Journal of Urban and Regional Research,
http://dx.doi.org/10.1111/j.1468-2427.2010.00956.x.

Ministère des Affaires Locales et de l'Environnement (2017), Portail des Collectivités Locales en Tunisie, http://www.collectiviteslocales.gov.tn/ (accessed on 29 January 2018).

Ministère du Développement, D. (2015), Développement de l'investissement local et gouvernance territoriale : Etat des lieux en Tunisie,
http://www.tunisieindustrie.nat.tn/fr/download/news/Jedile/05.pdf (accessed on 29 January 2018).

Neveu, C. (2011), "Démocratie participative et mouvements sociaux : entre domestication et ensauvagement ?", Participations, Vol. 1/1, p. 186, http://dx.doi.org/10.3917/parti.001.0186.

Nicolás Adán, J.E., Ben Hassen, S. & Doggui, A. (2014), Les cadres formels de concertation : un instrument efficace pour enraciner la démocratie participative en Tunisie,
http://eeas.europa.eu/archives/delegations/tunisia/documents/cultural_activities/pasc3_cadres_democratie_fr.pdf (accessed on 29 January 2018).

OCDE((n.d.)), Regional Demography, OECD.Statistics,
http://stats.oecd.org/Index.aspx?DataSetCode=REGION_DEMOGR (accessed on 30 January 2018).

OECD (2017a), Recommendation of the Council on Open Government http://acts.oecd.org (accessed on 29 January 2018).

OECD (2017b), Recommendation of the Council on Public Integrity
http://www.oecd.org/gov/ethics/OECD-Recommendation-Public-Integrity.pdf (accessed on 30 January 2018).

OECD (2016) Open Government: The Global Context and the Way Forward, OECD Publishing, Paris, https://doi.org/10.1787/9789264268104-en

OECD (2009), Focus on Citizens : Public Engagement for Better Policy and Services, OECD Publishing, Paris, https://doi.org/10.1787/9789264048874-en

Robert, D. (2016), "Une société civile tunisienne formatée ?", Nawaat, https://nawaat.org/portail/2016/06/13/une-societe-civile-tunisienne-formatee/ (accessed on 29 January 2018).

Schauppenlehner-Kloyber, E. and M. Penker (2016), "Between Participation and Collective Action— From Occasional Liaisons towards Long-Term Co-Management for Urban Resilience", Sustainability, Vol. 8/7, p. 664, http://dx.doi.org/10.3390/su8070664.

Shah, A. (2007), "Participatory Budgeting", Public Sector Governance and Accountability Series, https://www.unicef.org/spanish/socialpolicy/files/Participatory_Budgetting_Shah07.pdf (accessed on 29 January 2018).

Transparency International Lithuania (n.d.), Savivaldybiu Skaidrumo Vertinimas, http://www.jurgiokepure.lt/2015-2019/vilniaus-miesto (accessed on 30 January 2018).

Turki, S. and Verdeil, E. (2015), "Tunisie: la Constitution (du Printemps) Ouvre le Débat sur la Décentralisation", dans *Local Governments and Public Goods: Assessing Decentralization in the Arab World*, LCPS, https://halshs.archives-ouvertes.fr/halshs-01221381/document (accessed 29 January 2018).

UCLG, O. (2016), "Tunisia", http://www.oecd.org/regional/regional-policy/profile-tunisia.pdf (accessed on 30 January 2018).

Vie associative- Portail des associations d'Aubervilliers (n.d.), Subvention municipale, http://associations.aubervilliers.fr/le-soutien-aux-associations/subvention-municipale/ (accessed on 30 January 2018).

Notes

[1] www.cgdr.nat.tn/upload/files/13.pdf

[2] Municipality of Sayada - Decree No. 2011-1208 of 27 August 2011

[3] Government decree No. 2017-200 of 8 February 2017

[4] Decree No. 2011-694 of 9 June 2011

[5] Decree No. 2011-384 of 8 April 2011

[6] Decree No. 2012-2364 of 11 October 2012

[7] Government decree No. 2017-434 of 12 April 2017

[8] Documentation provided by the municpality of La Marsa

[9] www.legislation.tn/sites/default/files/files/textes_soumis_avis/texte/code-amenagement.pdf

[10] www.communemarsa.tn/e-reclamation

[11] www.facebook.com/pg/RadioLaMarsa/videos

Chapter 4. Conclusion and next steps

First and foremost, it should be noted that an opportune moment exists for Tunisia's municipalities to implement open government practices. Indeed, they can draw on a new legal framework and the commitment of associations and the municipalities themselves. Secondly, the current context – the legal framework and regional disparities – leaves them no choice other than to try fresh approaches to governance that place citizens at the heart of the process and promote the development of public policies closer to their needs.

To establish open government at the local level, the national government is called upon to set in place an enabling environment, through a clear and stable legal and institutional framework and suitable human and financial resources. The national government could also support the development of open government practices at the local level, drawing inspiration from its experiences in this area and offering guides, training and technical support. However, close coordination with organisations representing the municipalities remains a prerequisite, so as to take into account their needs and specific features and to create synergies between efforts at the national and local levels.

For their part, the municipalities could draw lessons from their current experiences and, based on the new legal framework, develop open government visions and strategies that include a roadmap, priority activities and performance indicators. These strategies would enable to reach a consensus with the citizens and civil society, and to define a vision that goes beyond electoral mandates.

Box 4.1. Summary of recommendations

Recommendations for central government

- The implementation and concretisation of the decentralisation process remains the key element for open government at the local level. Implementing the Code for Local Authorities and the accompanying laws would help to clearly define the decentralisation model chosen and the competences attributed at the subnational level. Increased legitimacy, competences and resources would enable local administrations to develop long-term approaches, thereby regaining the trust of citizens. This requires inter-ministerial coordination between the Ministry of Local Affairs and Environment, the Ministry of Finance and the Presidency of the Government, particularly the department responsible for open government, so as to ensure harmonisation between public policies for local development and decentralisation, and human and financial resources. These ministries could propose an institutional organisation that creates an appropriate institutional framework at the local level for open government, in which different departments and their officials responsible for respectively access to information, complaints, and the citizens' affairs office work in partnership and share information. Such a proposition for organising the institutional framework concerning open government tasks would help to ensure consistency. These structures should nevertheless be adapted to the municipalities' size and context.

- With the aim of better targeting Tunisia's national open government programme and making it an engine for the country's development, it would be useful to design structures to involve local government in national projects, such as the Steering Committee for Open Government or in the open data initiatives.

- Similarly, in order to strengthen and improve national programmes, such as the PDUGL, which aims to establish open government at the local level, it could prove valuable to involve local administrations to a greater extent, and to draw inspiration from processes and mechanisms developed at the local level. A closer involvement of local administrations, particularly through representative institutions (the future High Council of Local Authorities and the National Federation of Tunisian Cities), would enable programmes to be better adapted to local needs and conditions, and would encourage political commitment on the part of local actors.

- Taking into account the current situation and the recruitment freeze, the national government, in partnership with civil society and organisations representing the municipalities, could propose training in open government and access to information, in order to support municipalities in accomplishing their objectives. This process will require the involvement of various actors, such as the National School of Administration, or the International Academy for Good Governance.

Recommendations for the municipalities

- The municipalities could develop their own open government strategy at the local level. The mayors and elected representatives could, in consultation with the citizens, reach a consensus on the key priorities in the areas of transparency, stakeholder participation, integrity and accountability, drawing inspiration from the new prerogatives in the Code for Local Authorities. Such a strategy would include the vision, objectives and activities to be undertaken, as well as a calendar and indicators for an impact assessment. An open government strategy would enable a long-term approach to be taken, beyond the elections, and ensure consistency over the entire range of activities, while grouping together all the stakeholders around the same vision. It would also help to align the activities more closely with the human and financial resources available, and to draw up a roadmap to develop these resources. Strategies could be developed for each municipality, and exchanges could be useful for their harmonisation, so that the municipalities could learn from each other and adopt a joint approach towards central government.

- Similarly, in a spirit of openness and responsiveness to citizens' needs and expectations, the municipalities could consider engaging in dialogue with civil society to establish a common charter/vision, based on the charter adopted for the participatory budget. They could draft a roadmap to apply the clauses on open government included in the Code for Local Authorities. They could also consider other initiatives in the area of citizen participation, which go beyond participatory budgeting.

- It would be useful to draw lessons learned and best practices from existing practices, so that these experiences, as well as the trust built through the participatory budgeting process and the partnership in Sayada, may serve as a foundation for implementing structured mechanisms for public consultation and dialogue with all stakeholders affected by major municipal projects and urban development plans. More structured participation gains even more importance with the adoption of the Code for Local Authorities and the transfer of new competences to the municipalities.

- The municipalities are called on to develop open governance approaches that require few human and financial resources. Partnerships with civil society, universities or the private sector – such as those set up in Sayada to manage the website – could be considered. These partnerships could also serve to better target open government initiatives, working together to identify the most essential and often requested information and data, with the aim of ensuring their proactive publication, and with the aim of establishing a culture of transparency. Workshops and training sessions, as well as taking advantage of information and communication technologies, could help to create understanding of rights and obligations linked to access to information.

- Following the elections of May 2018, training and capacity development are crucial for the newly elected representatives, in order to promote a culture of local democracy; capacity building for public officials to help them develop policies in this area is also important.

- Since the municipal elections, the municipal councils and their committees have increased legitimacy and, as a result, they have become important venues for municipal decision-making. The municipalities could therefore strengthen their efforts to use information and communication technologies, especially social media networks, to increase participation, particularly in municipal council meetings.

- To build greater trust with citizens and civil society, it would be useful to increase transparency surrounding municipal operations, especially regarding delays in project implementation. This process requires a systematic approach of monitoring and evaluating project implementation.

- At a time when community radio, including web radio stations, is emerging in Tunisia, as well as online press, local authorities would do well to promote dialogue with these media channels to help them become active players in discussions between society and government. By making press contacts and facilitating direct access to information – without having to pass through the central government – municipalities can encourage a type of journalism that pays closer attention to local issues.

- Promoting the sharing of experiences and inter-municipal cooperation in the area of open government, through the National Federation of Tunisian Cities, through the organisation of a dedicated annual day and open government debates, would facilitate the development strategies and initiatives on this issue.

- Ensuring continuous monitoring and evaluation of open government strategies and initiatives at the local level would help to adapt these and strengthen their impact.

Recommendations for civil society, citizens and the media

- Civil society actors and the media could, in turn, build trust and dialogue by demonstrating greater transparency by adopting the best practices of internal governance, integrity and transparency in the management of their activities.

- They could also become policy advocates, proposing local authorities mechanisms for consultation and participation and playing the role of watchdog.

- They also play an important role in civic education on the new prerogatives of the Local Government Code and on access to information

ORGANISATION FOR ECONOMIC CO-OPERATION AND DEVELOPMENT

The OECD is a unique forum where governments work together to address the economic, social and environmental challenges of globalisation. The OECD is also at the forefront of efforts to understand and to help governments respond to new developments and concerns, such as corporate governance, the information economy and the challenges of an ageing population. The Organisation provides a setting where governments can compare policy experiences, seek answers to common problems, identify good practice and work to co-ordinate domestic and international policies.

The OECD member countries are: Australia, Austria, Belgium, Canada, Chile, the Czech Republic, Denmark, Estonia, Finland, France, Germany, Greece, Hungary, Iceland, Ireland, Israel, Italy, Japan, Korea, Latvia, Lithuania, Luxembourg, Mexico, the Netherlands, New Zealand, Norway, Poland, Portugal, the Slovak Republic, Slovenia, Spain, Sweden, Switzerland, Turkey, the United Kingdom and the United States. The European Union takes part in the work of the OECD.

OECD Publishing disseminates widely the results of the Organisation's statistics gathering and research on economic, social and environmental issues, as well as the conventions, guidelines and standards agreed by its members.

OECD PUBLISHING, 2, rue André-Pascal, 75775 PARIS CEDEX 16

(42 2018 59 1 P) ISBN 978-92-64-31098-8 – 2019

Printed by Libri Plureos GmbH in Hamburg, Germany